Behavioural Medicine

Guest editors

Andrew Mathews

and

Andrew Steptoe

The British Psychological Society

Published by The British Psychological Society
Headquarters St Andrews House, 48 Princess Road East, Leicester LE1 7DR, UK
Distribution Centre Blackhorse Road, Letchworth, Herts SG6 1HN, UK

First published, without an index, in British Journal of Clinical Psychology, volume 21, November
1982 – A publication of The British Psychological Society

ISBN 0 901715 19 0

Printed in Great Britain by Prototype Ltd., 62 Bell Road, Sittingbourne, Kent

Contents*

*Page numbers all refer to numbering in square brackets at the head of every page.

British Journal of Clinical Psychology (1982), **21**, 239–240   *Printed in Great Britain*

Editorial

The term 'behavioural medicine' has been adopted in recent years to describe applications of the behavioural sciences to clinical problems outside the traditional psychiatric domain. Many procedures fall into this category, and the distinctions between behavioural medicine and disciplines such as medical psychology or psychosomatic medicine are far from clear (Schwartz & Weiss, 1978). An eclectic approach is taken in this Special Issue, so as to include contributions that do not conform to the narrower behaviourist orientation favoured elsewhere (Pomerlau & Brady, 1979; Surwit *et al.*, in press). Nevertheless, the applications described here all derive from principles established in experimental settings, and are primarily concerned with empirical relationships between observable behaviour and clinical disorders.

We have chosen to organize this Special Issue around three main themes: communication and health care, psychological factors in cardiovascular disorders, and the management of pain. In doing so, we are partly influenced by current research activity, but partly also by our belief that these are central areas in the development of behavioural medicine as a clinical discipline. Each of the areas is introduced with an invited review by an acknowledged expert, followed by a group of empirical reports that illustrate some specific directions clinical research is taking at present.

Philip Ley's pioneering work on communication in health care settings has led to the realization that poor communication is an extremely important source of patient dissatisfaction. Moreover, patient adherence to advice and treatment is adversely affected by inadequate communication. Since patient satisfaction and compliance with treatment is essential in virtually all areas of medicine, these issues are obvious — yet previously neglected — targets for psychological intervention and research. The accompanying articles reflect some of the issues touched on in Ley's review, and illustrate investigations into the nature and extent of communication in hospitals (by Marie Johnston), psychological differences among pregnant women and their effects on childbirth (by Brewin & Bradley), and the effects of different psychological interventions on surgical recovery (by Ridgeway & Mathews).

Cardiovascular disorders are of special interest to psychologists, because of the increasing evidence that personality and behavioural factors are involved in the aetiology of coronary heart disease and high blood pressure. Moreover, psychological and behavioural procedures can be utilized in the treatment or prevention of cardiovascular disease, and this area is reviewed by Derek Johnston. Johnston's own research has been consistently directed at the mechanisms underlying psychological control of cardiovascular variables, and the applications of such control to treatment methods. The following paper by Basler *et al.* is an example of clinical intervention in general practice, and so has additional implications for the settings in which behavioural methods may be adopted. Further advances will depend on a clearer understanding of the way in which emotional or other psychological factors contribute to the development of cardiovascular disorders, an issue addressed in the final paper of this section by Steptoe *et al.*

The last major area considered in the Special Issue is the measurement and management of pain using psychological principles. The work of Wilbert Fordyce has played a crucial role in enhancing our understanding of chronic pain and its treatment. In the present review, Dr Fordyce outlines some recent research supporting the role of learning factors in chronic pain behaviour. The many treatment studies arising from this and related research are reviewed in the following paper (by Linton); in common with other recent reviews, this concludes that while there are grounds for optimism, the value of psychological procedures in the management of many types of chronic pain has not yet been conclusively documented. Precise measurement is one key to the development and evaluation of more effective treatments, and the paper by Dr Reading and others represents a contribution to the methodology of pain meaurement first developed by Melzack.

Finally, we think that clinical psychologists will find much of interest in the paper by William Redd, reviewing his own work with cancer patients. This illustrates some novel applications of operant principles, while also raising many professional and ethical problems concerning behavioural interventions with terminally ill patients. In conclusion, we hope that this collection of papers provides a useful and informative survey of some of the more promising developments in behavioural medicine, while at the same time serving to encourage clinical psychologists and their medical colleagues to enter this expanding field.

References

Pomerleau, O. F. & Brady, J. P. (eds) (1979). *Behavioral Medicine: Theory and Practice*. Baltimore: Williams & Wilkins.

Schwartz, G. E. & Weiss, S. M. (1978). Yale conference on behavioural medicine: A proposed definition and statement of goals. *Journal of Behavioral Medicine,* **1**, 3–12.

Surwit, R. S., Williams, R. B., Steptoe, A. & Biersner, R. (eds) (in press). *Behavioral Medicine: Behavioral Treatment of Disease*. New York: Plenum.

Andrew Mathews,
Professor of Psychology

Andrew Steptoe,
Senior Lecturer in Psychology

St George's Hospital Medical School, University of London.

British Journal of Clinical Psychology (1982), **21**, 241 – 254   *Printed in Great Britain*

Satisfaction, compliance and communication

Philip Ley

The literature on communication, compliance, and patient satisfaction is selectively reviewed. As in earlier reviews, it is concluded that dissatisfaction with communication remains widespread, as does lack of compliance with medical advice. Related factors include poor transmission of information from patient to doctor, low understandability of communications addressed to the patient, and low levels of recall of information by patients. There does not appear to be any evidence that provision of additional information leads to adverse reactions by patients. Theoretical approaches to communication and compliance are described, and it is concluded that these should be used to direct future research.

This review will attempt to provide an overview of current research and theory in the field of doctor – patient communication. It will focus on the relationships between communication, compliance and satisfaction and on methods for improving communication. Even with these limitations it will not be possible to provide an exhaustive review but the interested reader should find enough leads to most aspects of the field.

Probably the main exclusion is the effect of pre-operative communication on post-operative recovery. This area is discussed elsewhere in the issue by Ridgeway & Mathews. Also excluded are the areas of health education via the mass media (e.g. Green, 1980), communications between health care professions (Fletcher, 1973) and the encouragement of blood donation (Ostwalt, 1979).

The topics included have presented a major difficulty in that there is no obvious sequence for them. The final decision was to make the section on each topic as self-contained as possible to reduce the importance of order. The topics included are (1) patients' satisfaction; (2) compliance with advice; (3) the transmission of information from patient to doctor; (4) understandability of health communications; (5) recall of medical information; (6) potentially harmful effects of fuller information for patients; and (7) theoretical approaches.

Patients' satisfaction

A great deal of research into the relationships between communication, satisfaction and other variables has been conducted. Thus a satisfaction variable of some sort has figured in the researches of Ley, Korsch and Hulka. Ley has been concerned with satisfaction with communications, e.g. Ley *et al.* (1976*a*), Korsch with satisfaction with the consultation, e.g. Korsch *et al.* (1968), and Hulka with a composite satisfaction index made up of three components namely satisfaction with (*a*) professional competence, (*b*) personal qualities of the physician, and (*c*) costs and convenience of care (Hulka, 1979).

No investigation has simultaneously used all three measures of satisfaction devised by those three workers, but, with the emergence of more psychometrically sophisticated satisfaction questionnaires, research has been conducted which makes it seem likely that satisfaction with communications is a strong determinant of more general satisfaction with the medical encounter (Ware & Snyder, 1975; Dimatteo *et al.*, 1979; Mangelsdorff, 1979; Roghmann *et al.*, 1979).

Frequency of dissatisfaction

Ley (1972*a*, 1982*a*) has summarized investigations of dissatisfaction with communications, and Korsch *et al.* have reported on the frequency of dissatisfaction with consultation. The results of these investigations are shown in Table 1.

0144-6657/82/040241 – 14 $02.00/0 © 1982 The British Psychological Society

Table 1. Patients' satisfaction with communications and with consultation

Investigations		Satisfaction variable	Dissatisfied (%)	
(a)	British hospital in-patients 1960–1970 (Ley, 1972a)	Communication	Mdn Range	35 11–65
	1971–1979 (Ley, 1982a)	Communication	Mdn Range	53 18–65
(b)	British general practice patients (Ley, 1982a)	Communication	Mdn Range	35 21–51
(c)	British psychiatric in-patients Raphael & Peers (1972)	Communication	Mdn Range	39 31–54
(d)	Various USA patient groups (Ley, 1982a)	Communication	Mdn Range	36 8–51
(e)	Korsch et al. (1968)	Consultation as a whole	Highly Moderately	40 36

Hulka's measure of satisfaction yields scores as a continuous variable so her results cannot be summarized in this way.

Correlates of satisfaction

Patients' satisfaction with the consultation (Francis et al., 1969), satisfaction with communications (Kincey et al., 1975; Ley et al., 1976b; Ley, 1979a) and general satisfaction with medical care received (Haynes et al., 1979) all correlate with patients' compliance with advice. Satisfied patients are more likely to comply.

Patients' reports of their understanding of what they have been told have also been found to correlate with satisfaction with communications (Ley, 1979a). In addition Ley et al. (1976a) have reported an experiment with medical in-patients in which increased understanding led to increased satisfaction with communications, although this was not true of surgical patients. However Hulka et al. (1975a) report little if any relationship between patients' understanding and overall satisfaction.

Evidence of a correlation between satisfaction variables and retention of medical information had been provided by Bertakis (1977), Brody (1980) and Cassileth et al. (1980). Bertakis and Brody found that the amount recalled by patients was correlated with degree of satisfaction with the physician and with communications. Further, Bertakis found that a procedure successfully used to increase recall also increased satisfaction, thus providing both correlational and experimental evidence of the relationship. Cassileth et al. found that patients who felt that they had been told the right amount recalled more than other patients.

Several other variables have been found to correlate with satisfaction. These include the doctor being seen as (1) friendly rather than business-like; (2) understanding the patients' concerns and (3) not thwarting the patients' expectations (Korsch et al., 1968).

Compliance with advice

A variety of methods have been used for measuring patients' compliance with advice. These have been reviewed in detail by Gordis (1979) and Dunbar (1979, 1980). In the case of compliance with medication regimens these have been classified by Ley (1979b) as: self-report; pill counts; blood and urine tests; measures of outcome; and mechanical. In the case of compliance with clinic appointments the criterion is, obviously enough, actual clinic attendance. In general it appears that more people will be judged non-compliant by urine and blood tests than by pill counts, and more judged non-compliant by pill counts than by self-report. Measures of outcome are used mainly in studies of compliance by diabetics, hypertensives and the obese.

Reviews of percentages of patients complying with medication regimens have been provided by Ley (1976), Food and Drug Administration (1979) and Barofsky (1980). The findings of these reviews are summarized in Table 2.

Table 2. The frequency with which patients fail to take their medication properly

Type of medication	Patients non-compliant (%)		
	Ley (1976)	Food & Drug Administration (1979)	Barofsky (1980)
Antibiotics	49	48	52
Psychiatric	39	42	42
Anti-hypertensive	–	43	61
Anti-tuberculosis	38	42	43
Other medications	48	54	46

The problem seems to be a general one and not just confined to medication, in that non-compliance with other forms of medical advice seems to be high as well. Ley (1976) reported mean percentage of non-compliance being 49 per cent for diets, and 51 per cent for other forms of advice. Ley (1978) reported a median drop-out rate of 48 per cent for 14 slimming clinics, although drop-outs from behaviour modification slimming programmes seem lower, having a median of 12 per cent for the studies reviewed by Hall & Hall (1974), and 21 per cent for clinics run for non-student clients in the community (Ley, 1980a). Not all compliance studies lend themselves to tabular summary of the sort used here. Exhaustive annotated bibliographies of such investigation have been provided in the excellent review books edited by Sackett & Haynes (1976) and Haynes *et al.* (1979). In addition there is an increasing number of reviews devoted to compliance in a restricted area of medicine, e.g. hypertension (Haynes *et al.*, 1980), ophthamology (Ashburn *et al.*, 1980).

It should not necessarily be assumed that compliance is desirable. Ley (1977) has suggested that it is desirable only after genuine informed consent has been obtained, and provided that there are opportunities for the patient to withdraw that informed consent. Fuller discussion of the ethical issues involved can be found in Stimson (1974) and Jonsen (1979). The ethical problem is further complicated by the findings that health care professionals do not always themselves comply with the best available recommendations about health, even when issuing advice to patients. Ley (1981) reported rates of non-compliance of this sort ranging from 12 to 95 per cent with a median of 80 per cent; and that 51 – 100 per cent of patients (median 65 per cent) do not receive appropriate medication or advice about it.

The costs of non-compliance have also been estimated. The US Food and Drug Administration (1979) provided estimates of financial costs. A different approach is to estimate the proportion of hospitalized patients whose hospitalization can be attributed to non-compliance. Ausburn (1981) reported such an investigation, in which she found that in 20 per cent of patients admission was probably, and in another 5 per cent possibly, due to non-compliance with medication regimens.

Correlates of non-compliance
Attempts have been made to delineate the non-compliant patient's individual or social characteristics, (Ley 1976). Ley (1979b) has summarized the findings of such studies as

showing that *none* of the following is related to non-compliance: the patients' sociodemographic or personality characteristics; the doctor's characteristics; illness variables, including duration and severity of the illness.

Variables which do seem to be related to non-compliance include: duration and complexity of regimen; patients' levels of dissatisfaction; lack of supportive follow-up; patients' perceptions of their vulnerability to the consequences of the illness, the seriousness of the illness, the effectiveness of treatment, and problems caused by treatment. This last group of variables includes many from the Health Belief Model which is discussed further below. In addition to these variables there are other possibilities. Ley (1979b), for example, suggested that with some medications, state-dependency effects and motivational effects could occur as a result of taking the drug. Finally it is worth noting that although both patients and their physicians believe that the experience of side-effects decreases compliance, the objective evidence fails to support this belief (Haynes *et al.,* 1979).

Reducing non-compliance

Several remedies have been suggested for non-compliance, including educational, persuasive and behaviour modification strategies. Educational strategies have ranged from the simple provision of written information about the treatment (Morris & Halperin, 1979), to major attempts to educate patients about their illness and the rationale of treatment (Roth, 1979).

Morris & Halperin (1979) reviewed investigations of the effects of written information and found that in the case of short-term medication (mainly anti-microbial) six out of seven investigations reported greater compliance in groups receiving written information. In the case of long-term treatment, only six out of 11 studies reported greater compliance.

Persuasive strategies do not appear to have been much used. In fact Haynes *et al.* (1979) in their annotated bibliography list only three references in this area, and they are all on fear arousal. The only series of experiments attempting to reduce non-compliance by the application of social psychological findings concerning persuasive communications is that of Ley and his co-workers (Ley *et al.,* 1974; Skilbeck *et al.,* 1977; Ley 1978; Ley *et al.,* 1979). These investigations have manipulated traditional variables such as fear level, sidedness and frequency of exposure, in messages designed to help women adhere to slimming regimens. Few if any firm findings have emerged, but several of the variables investigated have had significant effects on at least some occasions, e.g. degree of fear aroused in subjects; sidedness of argument; frequency of exposure to fear appeals; and position of fear appeals in the message.

Behaviour modification strategies are being increasingly used to reduce non-compliance and have included: self-monitoring; monetary reinforcement; token reinforcement; behavioural contracts; and aversive procedures. A review of these and their effectiveness has been provided by Dunbar *et al.* (1979). At this stage it is not possible to draw firm conclusions about their usefulness, but there have been some interesting successes, e.g. Azrin & Powell (1969), Baile & Engel (1978), Epstein & Masek (1978), Dapcich-Miura & Hovell (1979).

In some ways perhaps the wisest method of increasing patients' compliance is to discover the features in the particular situation which are contributing to non-compliance and then do something appropriate about them. An excellent example of this can be found in the work of Finnerty's team (Finnerty *et al.,* 1973a, b). These investigators found that waiting time, lack of 24-hour availability, and variations in staff seen on different visits seemed to be contributing to a 42 per cent clinic drop-out rate. When these factors were attended to, the drop-out rate was reduced to 8 per cent.

The transmission of information from patient to doctor

It seems probable that in many clinical situations, patients do not always provide their doctors with full accounts of their symptoms and problems. For example, Korsch *et al.* (1968) found that 65 per cent of the expectations held by the patients they studied were not mentioned to the physician, nor were 76 per cent of the patients' main worries.

There are a number of reasons why the doctor should fail to elicit information from the patient. These include: patients' diffidence; poor interviewing technique on the part of the doctor; and doctors' feelings of discomfort in interviews.

Patients' diffidence is an often mentioned but little researched problem (Ley, 1972*a*; Roter, 1977). Carstairs (1970) found that 53 – 67 per cent of patients were too diffident to voice complaints on various topics. More recently Roter (1977) has conducted an experimental investigation of this problem. Patients were interviewed before consulation to find out what information they wished to acquire from the physician. If necessary they were taught how to word questions. This was effective in increasing the number of questions asked, but led to an increase in anxiety and anger during the consultation, and higher patient dissatisfaction. Interestingly it also led to greater compliance in attending follow-up consultations.

Errors of interviewing techniques have been discussed by a multitude of authors, some of whom have suggested ways in which matters could be improved, e.g. Maguire & Rutter (1976); Fletcher (1980). If the interviewing skills of doctors are as deficient as these reviews suggest, the solutions must be (*a*) to provide more training in this area for trainee doctors, and (*b*) to provide instruction and advice to already qualified doctors.

Maguire and his colleagues have investigated the effectiveness of an interview training technique based on their own and previous research into common interviewing errors. The procedure has been shown to successfully increase the amount of useful information elicited by the interviewer (Rutter & Maguire, 1976; Maguire, 1979).

Inui *et al.* (1976) and Ley *et al.* (1976*a*) evaluated the effects of providing information to experienced doctors, hospital physicians in the first case and general practitioners in the second. Inui *et al.* provided their physicians with a single tutorial session designed to make the physicians better as managers and educators of hypertensive patients. Patients whose physicians had attended the tutorial acquired greater knowledge of their illness, were more compliant and achieved better control of their hypertension. Ley *et al.* investigated the effects of providing general practitioners with a list of empirically based suggestions for improving communication. It was found that use of the suggestions resulted in patients retaining more of the information that they had been given. While neither of these studies was directly concerned with the elicitation of information from patients, they do demonstrate that the communicative behaviour of experienced doctors can sometimes be changed to advantage.

With regard to difficulties of communication as perceived by medical practitioners it has been found that problems were presented in dealing with three categories of patient (1) husband and wife attending together (2) adolescents (3) medically trained people (Bennett *et al.*, 1978). Some situations also made for communications difficulties. The commonest were consultations involving: (1) drug dependencies (2) the possibility of child abuse (3) refusing requests for a certificate or prescription. For present purposes the most interesting finding was that these doctors perceived the task of discovering the patients' reason for attendance as being the area where they had most communication difficulties. Using a more direct approach in which doctors filled in questionnaires about a consultation just after it had finished, Pendleton (1979) reported that five variables seemed to be associated with the doctor feeling that a consultation had been problematic. These were (1) the patient was seen as being tense (2) the doctor not feeling relaxed (3) the patient being of lower social class (4) the patient having often consulted previously with the particular complaint (5) the patient being younger.

Understandability of health communications

Ley (1980*b*) has suggested three main criteria for judging the understandability of communications addressed to patients. These are (1) patients' self-report of understanding; (2) behavioural or quasi-behavioural tests; (3) readability measures.

As judged by each of these criteria, communications frequently fail to be understood. Patients' self-reports indicate that 7 – 53 per cent do not understand what they have been told (Ley, 1980*b*). Patient self-report is of course prone to the error of the patient wrongly thinking that he has understood when in fact he has not. It is not surprising therefore that even larger percentages of patients are judged not to have understood by behavioural tests. These have been concerned with following instructions or medication regimens and it has been found that 53 – 89 per cent do not understand as judged by this method (Ley, 1982*a*).

Readability formulas purport to allow estimation of the percentage of the population who would understand written material. For brief details of these see Ley (1973, 1977). Several investigations have applied readability formulae to written material produced for patients. The results of these investigations are shown in Table 3.

Table 3. Understandability of written information for patients

Materials	Number of leaflets which would be understood by stated per cent of population:			
	25% or less	26 – 40%	41 – 74%	75% or more
X-ray leaflets (Ley *et al.*, 1972)	—	2	—	3
Dental leaflets (Ley, 1974)	1	1	—	3
Non-prescription drug leaflets (Pyrczak & Roth, 1976)	6	3	—	1
Prescription drug leaflets (Liguori, 1978)	—	3	—	1
Opticians' leaflets French *et al.*, 1978)	7	20	9	2
Cancer leaflets (DHEW, 1979)	6	2	—	—
Health education leaflets (Cole, 1979)	4	4	—	7
All of the above	24	35	9	17

Readability formulae should be used with caution for at least two reasons. Firstly, a high readability score can be quite compatible with a leaflet which is hard to understand. However a low score nearly always indicates that something is drastically wrong. Secondly, different formulas can yield different absolute difficulty levels, although the relative difficulty of a set of leaflets as judged by different formulae is usually the same (Ley, 1980*b*).

However, in the light of the above evidence it can be safely recommended that health care professionals should routinely apply a readability formula to written information they prepare for patients. Nor should psychologists feel that they are immune from producing written material of low readability for patients. Andrasik *et al.* (1977, 1981) have shown that both behaviour therapy manuals and self-report assertion inventories are often too difficult for general use.

Recall of medical information
Magnitude of forgetting

Investigations of patients' forgetting of material presented to them by doctors have now been conducted in a variety of settings, using patients with a variety of diagnoses as subjects. These are summarized in Table 4.

Table 4. Patients' forgetting of what their doctors have told them

		Type of patients	% forgotten
1. *General practice*			
Ley *et al.* (1973)		Mixed	50
Ley *et al.* (1976*b*)		Mixed	44
Bertakis (1977)		Mixed	38
2. *Medical out-patients*			
Ley & Spelman (1965)		Mixed	37
Ley & Spelman (1967)	(*a*)	Mixed	39
	(*b*)	Mixed	41
Joyce *et al.* (1969)	(*a*)	Rheumatological	52
	(*b*)	Rheumatological	54
Anderson (1979)		Rheumatological	60
Bergler *et al.* (1980)		Hypertensive	28
3. *Mixed out-patients*			
Cassileth *et al.* (1980)		Cancer	31
4. *Surgical in-patients and out-patients*			
Robinson & Merav (1976)		Cardiac surgery	71
Priluck *et al.* (1979)		Detached retina	43

Variations in percentages recalled are possibly due to individual differences (see below), or to more mundane procedural differences in the investigations. For example, the information to be recalled was presented orally in most studies but in written form in that of Cassileth *et al.* (1980). In addition, time elapsing between the presentation of the information and its recall has varied from almost no delay to four to six months delay. These and other procedural variations make the interpretation of differences in recall difficult.

It is also true that the data summarized in Table 4 were obtained after a single presentation of the information to be recalled. This raises the possibility that in conditions where there is prolonged and repeated contact with the physician recall might be higher. Relevant data have been provided by Hulka *et al.* (1975*a, b*) who found that diabetics, mothers of infant patients, and pregnant woman could recall respectively, 67 per cent, 88 per cent, and 68 per cent of what their doctors had told them. It is clear from these results that even with repeated contact with health care personnel patients will often forget what they have been told.

Correlates of forgetting

A consistent finding has been that the number of statements forgotten is correlated with the number of statements presented. Ley (1979*c*) presented a linear regression equation for predicting number of statements forgotten from number presented. Unfortunately this does not fit the data reported by Anderson (1979).

Age has not been consistently found to correlate with forgetting. Ley & Spelman (1965) found that older patients recalled *more* than younger ones, but a more common finding is that there is no relationship between age and forgetting (Joyce *et al.*, 1969; Anderson, 1979; Ley 1979*c*; Brody, 1980); except for the possibility that patients over 65 years of age might forget more (Ley *et al.,* 1976*b*; Anderson 1979). Intelligence measured directly or inferred from educational level has produced mixed findings, e.g. Brody (1980). However the better educated were found to recall more by Bertakis (1977), and Anderson *et al.* (1979).

The relationship between anxiety and recall has also been investigated. Ley & Spelman (1967) reported a Yerkes – Dodson type relationship between anxiety and recall, but Anderson (1979) found that the higher the anxiety the better the recall. Another individual difference correlate of recall is level of medical knowledge, high medical knowledge being associated with better recall (Ley, 1979*c*).

Ley & Spelman (1967) and others have found that category of statement was related to recall, diagnostic statements being best and instructions being worst recalled. This finding was shown to be probably due to primacy and perceived importance effects (Ley, 1972*b*). Not surprisingly therefore, the finding of better recall of diagnostic statements and worse recall of instructions is not universal (Joyce *et al.,* 1969; Bertakis, 1977; Anderson, 1979).

Table 5. Effects of memory-enhancing techniques on recall of medical information

Investigations	Material	Method	% improvement		P
Analogue studies					
Ley (1972*b*)	Medical statements	Primacy		+17	<0·01
Ley *et al.* (1972)	X-ray leaflets	Simplification	(*a*)	−6	n.s.
			(*b*)	+34	<0·01
Bradshaw *et al.* (1975)	Slimming advice	Simplification	(*a*)	+29	n.s.
			(*b*)	+72	<0·05
Ley (1982*b*)	Glaucoma leaflet	Simplification		+34	<0·001
Ley (1979*c*)	Medical statements (7 studies)	Explicit categorization		+31	<0·01
Ley (1979*c*)	Medical statements (6 studies)	Repetition		+31	<0·01
Bradshaw *et al.* (1975)	Slimming advice	Use of specific statements	(*a*)	+350	<0·001
			(*b*)	+158	<0·001
			(*c*)	+219	<0·001
Real-life studies					
Ley (1972*b*)	Advice statements	(*a*) Primary		+74	<0·01
		(*b*) Stressed importance		+38	<0·06
Ley *et al.* (1979)	Menopause booklet	Simplification		+27	<0·05
Ley *et al.* (1973)	Doctors' statements	Explicit categorization		+24	<0·01
Kupst *et al.* (1975)	Doctors' statements	Repetition	(*a*)	+20	<0·01
			(*b*)	+20²	<0·01
Bertakis (1977)	Doctors' statements	Repetition		+33	<0·001
Ley (1982*b*)	Pediatric leaflets	Adjunct questions		−20	n.s.
Ley *et al.* (1976*b*)	Doctors' statements	Mixture	(*a*)	+17	
			(*b*)	+20	<0·001
			(*c*)	+26	
			(*d*)	+36	
Ley *et al.* (1979)	Contraception booklet	Mixture		−6	n.s.

Control of patients' recall

Attempts to improve recall of medical information have involved both real-life and analogue studies. In general it seems to be true, even if somewhat surprising, that recall of fictitious medical information by volunteer subjects closely mirrors recall of true information by real patients (Ley & Spelman, 1967; Ley, 1972*b*).

The techniques studied have been: the use of primacy and perceived importance effects, simplification, explicit categorization, repetition, use of specific advice statements, use of adjunct questions and mixtures of the above. Some discussion of other possible techniques can be found in Ley (1980*b*).

The results of these investigations are shown in Table 5. These results are promising but still present some problems in that a given technique is not always successful in increasing recall. Further research is probably worthwhile in that increasing patients' recall might lead to reduced non-compliance, and is clearly of relevance to the current debate about informed consent.

The potentially harmful effects of fuller communication

Clinicians who oppose the provision of full or fuller information to patients often do so because they believe that such provision will lead to undesirable consequences. Thus patients with cancer, or who are likely to die soon, are often not told the nature of their condition on the grounds that they will be happier not knowing. Full information about less serious illness is often withheld because it is felt that to provide full information would only make the patient anxious or depressed. The risks and dangers of investigative procedures are often not disclosed on similar grounds, and in the case of medication the possibility of side-effects is not mentioned because to do so might either increase the probability of their occurrence or reduce compliance with the regimen.

In general, a clear majority (ranging from 66 to 93 per cent) of patients approved of being told that they had cancer or were going to die (Kelly & Friesen, 1950; Aitken-Swan & Easson, 1959; Gilbertsen & Wangensteen, 1962). Similarly, little or no evidence of increased depression or anxiety was reported when patients were given extra information about test results (Alfidi, 1971; Greenwood, 1973), even to the extent of being given access to their own case notes (Golodetz *et al.,* 1976; Stevens *et al.,* 1977; Fischbach *et al.,* 1980). Finally, fuller information about drugs does not appear to decrease compliance, nor does it increase side-effects (e.g. Myers & Calvert, 1973, 1976, 1978). It can be seen that on the evidence available the provision of fuller information does not usually lead to the predicted adverse reactions.

Theoretical approaches

Some theoretical models in this field are really lists or categorizations of variables which could affect compliance and/or satisfaction outcomes. Good examples of these are the Precede model of Green (1980), and the input – output communication – persuasion matrix of McGuire (1980).

Fishbein's & Ajzen's more dynamic, but still general, model has also been applied to compliance problems in the health field. The *theory of reasoned action* states that behaviour is determined largely by intentions. These in turn are determined by the actor's attitude to that behaviour, and by the actor's subjective norm about the behaviour. Attitude to the behaviour depends on beliefs that the behaviour leads to certain outcomes and the actor's evaluations of these outcomes. The subjective norm on the other hand, depends on the actor's beliefs about what specific individuals or groups think about his performing the behaviour, and his motivation to comply with these specific individuals and groups. The model is discussed in most detail in Fishbein & Ajzen (1975), but especially useful for those wishing to conduct research using this model is Ajzen & Fishbein (1980). Research into application of the model to health care problems has included alcoholics, the obese and smokers amongst its targets (Fishbein, 1976; Ajzen & Fishbein, 1980).

The best-established model in this field is however the *Health Belief Model.* This model sees the adoption of a health-promoting behaviour as being determined by (1) a cue to action, (2) perceived vulnerability to the health problem, (3) the perceived seriousness of the illness, (4) the perceived effectiveness of the treatment of advocated action, (5) the perceived costs of adopting the treatment or action. The basic model and some modifications of it have been reviewed by Becker (1976, 1979) and Ley (1979*b*). In terms of published results it seems well supported in most aspects. Unfortunately most of the research to date has been correlational rather than experimental, and there are too many investigations using retrospective rather than prospective measures of the main predictor variables for the firm drawing of conclusions about the model's likely utility in changing health behaviours. This point becomes particularly important in view of the findings reported by Becker *et al.* (1979) that in a trial of blood pressure reduction techniques, health beliefs measured before treatment started were not correlated with later compliance; correlations being found only for health beliefs measured at the same time as compliance. In fairness to the Health Belief Model it should perhaps be added that the same paper presents data on a study of obesity in which pre-treatment measures did correlate with outcome variables). Other criticisms of the model have been summarized by Leventhal *et al.* (1980).

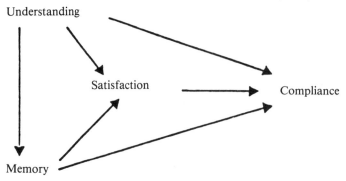

Figure 1. The cognitive hypothesis.

The cognitive model of communication and compliance first put forward by Ley & Spelman (1967) and elaborated by Ley (1980*b*, 1982*a*) is really only a partial model of satisfaction and compliance. The hypothesis claims that a significant proportion of the variance in both patient satisfaction and compliance can be accounted for by comprehension and memory variables. The model is summarized in Fig. 1.

Much of the relevant evidence has been reviewed above and much of this has been consistent with the model. However Ley (1979*b*, 1982*a*) has recognized that there are experimental studies such as Sackett *et al.* (1975), in which improvement of comprehension and memory has not led to the predicted drop in non-compliance. This has necessitated the elaboration of the model to include different types of non-compliant subjects. Non-compliers have been classified along two dimensions, (1) the adequacy and accuracy of their information and (2) whether their non-compliance is voluntary or involuntary. The effectiveness of increasing understanding of and memory for messages will depend on the type of non-complier who is the target. It should have no effect on voluntary non-compliers who have adequate information, but should have a large effect on involuntary non-compliers who have insufficient information. No direct tests of this modification have been attempted and there are obvious problems in the definition of adequacy of information.

Conclusions

It is quite obvious that the communication problems highlighted by Ley & Spelman (1967) are still in existence today. Patients remain dissatisfied with communication, often do not understand and often forget what they are told. Written information for patients continues to be produced in language too difficult for its intended audience. Finally, patients remain as non-compliant as ever.

New problems have also received attention, particularly the role of the doctor in obtaining information, and more recently the problem of non-compliance with the rules of good health care by health care professionals themselves.

Some solutions are also beginning to emerge. Methods for making clinicians better at both eliciting and presenting information have been discovered and tested. There is also a healthy and gowing interest in theoretical models, and with their development the (relatively) shotgun nature of much previous research will disappear from the scene. It is also of interest that much of the early research into patients' understanding and memory, conducted for its own sake, is proving to be highly relevant to current discussions of informed consent.

There are then grounds for optimism. Nevertheless it is sobering to realize that if the rates of non-compliance by health care professionals cited earlier are general, there is a high probability that clinicians will not comply with the suggestions for improved communications implicit in the findings of the studies reviewed here.

References

Aitken-Swan, J. & Easson, E. C. (1959). Reactions of cancer patients on being told their diagnosis. *British Medical Journal,* 1, 779–781.

Ajzen, I. & Fishbein, M. (1980). *Understanding Attitudes and Predicting Social Behaviour.* Englewood Cliffs, NJ: Prentice-Hall.

Alfidi, R. (1971). Informed consent: A study of patient reaction. *Journal of the American Medical Association,* 216, 1325–1329.

Anderson, J. L. (1979). Patients recall of information and its relation to the nature of the consultation. In D. Oborne, M. M. Gruneberg & J. R. Eiser (eds), *Research in Psychology and Medicine.* London: Academic Press.

Anderson, J. L., Dodman, S., Kopelman, M. & Fleming, A. (1979). Patient information recall in a rheumatology clinic. *Rheumatology and Rehabilitation,* 18, 18–22.

Andrasik, F. & Murphy, W. D. (1977). Assessing the readability of thirty-nine behaviour modification training manuals. *Journal of Applied Behaviour Analysis* 10, 341–344.

Andrasik, F. Heimberg, R. G., Edmund, R. S. & Blankenburg (1981). Assessing the readability level of self-report assertion inventories. *Journal of Consulting and Clinical Psychology,* 49, 142–144.

Ashburn, F. S. Goldberg, I. & Kass, M. A. (1980). Compliance with ocular therapy. *Survey of Ophthalmology,* 24, 237–248.

Ausburn, L. (1981). Patient compliance with medication regimens. In J. Sheppard (ed.), *Behavioural Medicine.* Lidcombe, NSW: Cumberland College of Health Sciences.

Azrin, N. H. & Powell, J. (1969). Behavioural engineering: The use of response priming to improve prescribed self-medication. *Journal of Applied Behaviour Analysis,* 2, 39–42.

Baile, W. F. & Engel, B. T. (1978). A behavioural strategy for promoting treatment compliance following myocardial infarction. *Psychosomatic Medicine,* 40, 413–419.

Barofsky, I. (1980). *The Chronic Psychiatric Patient in the Community.* New York: Plenum.

Becker, M. H. (1976). Sociobehavioural determinants of compliance. In D. L. Sackett & R. B. Haynes (eds), *Compliance with Therapeutic Regimens.* Baltimore: Johns Hopkins University Press.

Becker, M. H. (1979). Understanding patient compliance. In S. J. Cohen (ed.), *New Directions in Patient Compliance.* Lexington, MA: Lexington Books.

Becker, M. H., Maiman, L. A., Kirscht, J. P., Haefner, D. P., Drachman, R. H. & Taylor, D. W. (1979). Patient perceptions and compliance: Recent studies of the Health Belief Model. In R. B. Haynes, D. W. Taylor & D. L. Sackett (eds), *Compliance in Health Care.* Baltimore: Johns Hopkins University Press.

Bennett, A., Knox, J. D. E. & Morrison, A. T. (1978). Difficulties in consultations reported by doctors in general practice. *Journal of the Royal College of General Practitioners,* 28, 646–651.

Bergler, J. H., Pennington, A. C., Metcalfe, M. & Freis, E. D. (1980). Informed consent: How much does the patient understand? *Clinical Pharmacology and Therapeutics,* 27, 435–440.

Bertakis, K. D. (1977). The communication of information from physician to patient: A method for increasing retention and satisfaction. *Journal of Family Practice,* 5, 217–222.

Bradshaw, P. W., Ley, P., Kincey, J. A., & Bradshaw, J. (1975). Recall of medical advice: Comprehensibility and specificity. *British Journal of Social and Clinical Psychology,* 14, 55–62.

Brody, D. S. (1980). An analysis of patient recall of their therapeutic regimens. *Journal of Chronic Diseases,* 33, 57–63.

Carstairs, V. (1970). *Channels of Communication.* Edinburgh: Scottish Home and Health Department.

Cassileth, B. R., Zupkis, R. V., Sutton-Smith, K. & March, V. (1980). Informed consent — Why are its goals imperfectly realised? *New England Journal of Medicine,* 302, 896–900.

Cole, R. (1979). The understanding of medical terminology used in printed health educational materials. *Health Education Journal*, **38**, 111–121.

Dapcich-Miura, & Hovell, M. F. (1979). Contingency management to a complex medical regimen in an elderly heart patient. *Behaviour Therapy*, **10**, 193–201.

Department of Health Education and Welfare (1979). *Readability Testing in Cancer Communications.* Washington, DC: National Institutes of Health (NIH 79–1689).

Dimatteo, M.R., Prince, L.M. & Taranta, A. (1979). Patients perceptions of physicians behaviour. *Journal of Community Health*, **4**, 280–289.

Dunbar, J. M. (1979). Issues in assessment. In S. J. Cohen (ed.), *New Directions in Patient Compliance.* Lexington, MA: Lexington Books.

Dunbar, J. M. (1980). Assessment of medication compliance. In R. B. Haynes, M. E. Mattson & T. O. Engebretson (eds), *Patient Compliance to Prescribed Anti-hypertensive Medication Regimens.* Bethesda, MD: National Institutes of Health (NIH 81–2102).

Dunbar, J. M., Marshall, G. D. & Hovell, M. F. (1979). Behavioural strategies for improving compliance. In R. B. Haynes, D. W. Taylor & D. L. Sackett (eds), *Compliance in Health Care.* Baltimore: Johns Hopkins University Press.

Epstein, L. H. & Masek, B. J. (1978). Behavioural control of medicine compliance. *Journal of Applied Behaviour Analysis*, **11**, 1–9.

Finnerty, F. A., Mattie, E. C. & Finnerty, F. A. (1973a). Hypertension in the inner city: I. Analysis of clinic drop-outs. *Circulation*, **47**, 73–75.

Finnerty, F., Shaw, L. & Himmelsback, C. (1973b). Hypertension in the inner city: II: Detection and follow-up. *Circulation*, **47**, 76–78.

Fischbach, R. L., Bayog, A. S., Needle, A. & Delbanco, T. L. (1980). The patient and practitioner as co-authors of the medical record. *Patient Counselling and Health Education*, **2**, 1–5.

Fishbein, M. (1976). Persuasive communication. In A. E. Bennett (ed.), *Communication Between Doctors and Patients.* London: Oxford University Press for the Nuffield Provincial Hospitals Trust.

Fishbein, M. & Ajzen, I. (1975). *Belief, Attitude, Intention and Behaviour.* Reading, MA: Addison-Wesley.

Fletcher, C. (1973). *Communication in Medicine.* London: Nuffield Provincial Hospitals Trust.

Fletcher, C. (1980). Listening and talking to patients. 1. The problem. *British Medical Journal*, **281**, 845–847.

Food and Drug Administration (1979). Prescription drug products: Patient labelling requirements. *Federal Register*, **44**, 40016–40041.

Food and Drug Administration (1980). Prescription drug products: Patient package insert requirements. *Federal Register*, **45**, 60754–60780.

Francis, V., Korsch, B. M. & Morris, M. J. (1969). Gaps in doctor–patient communication: Patients response to medical advice. *New England Journal of Medicine*, **280**, 535–540.

French, C., Mellor, M. & Parry, L. (1978). Patients view of the ophthalmic optician. *The Ophthalmic Optician*, 28 October, 784–786.

Gilbertsen, V. A. & Wangensteen, O. H. (1962). Should the doctor tell the patient the disease is cancer? *Ca*, **12**, 82–86.

Golodetz, A. Ruess, J. & Michaus, R. L. (1976). The right to know: Giving the patient his medical record. *Archives of Physical Medicine and Rehabilitation*, **57**, 78–81.

Gordis, L. (1979). Conceptual and methodological problems in measuring patient compliance. In R. B. Haynes, D. W. Taylor & D. L. Sackett (eds), *Compliance in Health Care.* Baltimore: Johns Hopkins University Press.

Green, L. W. (1980). *Health Education Planning: A Diagnostic Approach.* Palo Alto, CA: Mayfield.

Greenwood, R. D. (1973). Should the patient be informed of innocent murmurs? *Clinical Pediatrics*, **12**, 468–477.

Hall, S. M. & Hall, R. G. (1974). Outcome and methodological considerations in behavioural treatments of obesity. *Behaviour Therapy*, **5**, 352–364.

Haynes, R. B., Mattson, M. E. & Engebretson, T.O. (1980). *Patient Compliance to Prescribed Anti-hypertensive Medication Regimens: A Report to the National Heart, Lung and Blood Insitute.* Bethesda, MD: National Institutes of Health (NIH 81–2102).

Haynes, R. B., Taylor, D. W. & Sackett, D. L. (1979). *Compliance in Health Care.* Baltimore: Johns Hopkins University Press.

Hulka, B. S. (1979). Patient–clinician interaction and compliance. In R. B. Haynes, D. W. Taylor & D. L. Sackett (eds), *Compliance in Health Care,* Baltimore: Johns Hopkins University Press.

Hulka, B., Kupper, L., Cassel, J., Efird, R. & Burdette, J. (1975a). Medication use and misuse: Physician–patient discrepancies. *Journal of Chronic Diseases*, **28**, 7–21.

Hulka, B. S., Kupper, L., Cassel, J. C. & Mayo, F. (1975b). Doctor–patient communication and outcomes among diabetic patients. *Journal of Community Health,* **1**, 15–27.

Inui, T. S., Yourtree, E. L. & Williamson, J. W. (1976). Improved outcomes in hypertension after physician tutorials: A controlled trial. *Annals of Internal Medicine*, **84**, 646–651.

Jonsen, A. R. (1979). Ethical problems in compliance. In R. B. Haynes, D. W. Taylor & D. L. Sackett (eds), *Compliance in Health Care.* Baltimore: Johns Hopkins University Press.

Joyce, C. R. B., Caple G., Mason, M., Reynolds, E. & Mathews, J. A. (1969). Quantitative study of doctor–patient communication. *Quarterly Journal of Medicine*, **38**, 183–194.

Kelly, W. D. & Freisen, S. R. (1950). Do cancer patients want to be told? *Surgery*, **27**, 822–826.

Kincey, J. A., Bradshaw, P. W. & Ley, P. (1975). Patients satisfaction and reported acceptance of advice in general practice. *Journal of the Royal College of General Practitioners,* **25**, 558–566.

Korsch, B. M., Gozzi, E. K. & Francis, V. (1968). Gaps in doctor–patient communication: Doctor–patient interaction and patient satisfaction. *Pediatrics,* **42**, 855–871.

Kupst, M. J., Dresser, K., Schulman, J. L. & Paul, M. H. (1975). Evaluation of methods to improve communication in the physician–patient relationship. *American Journal of Orthopsychiatry,* **45**, 420–429.

Leventhal, H., Meyer, D., Gutmann, M. (1980). The role of theory on the study of compliance to high blood pressure regimens. In R. B. Haynes, M. E. Mattson & T. O. Engebretson (eds), *Patient Compliance to Prescribed Anti-hypertensive Medication Regimens.* Bethesda, MD: National Institutes of Health (NIH 81–2102).

Ley, P. (1972a). Complaints by hospital staff and patients: A review of the literature. *Bulletin of The British Psychological Society,* **25**, 115–120.

Ley, P. (1972b). Primacy, rated importance and the recall of medical information. *Journal of Health and Social Behaviour,* **13**, 311–317.

Ley, P. (1973). The measurement of comprehensibility. *Journal of the Institute of Health Education,* **11**, 17–20.

Ley, P. (1974). Communication in the clinial setting. *British Journal of Orthodontics,* **1**, 173–177.

Ley, P. (1976). Towards better doctor–patient communication: Contributions from social and experimental psychology. In A. E. Bennett (ed.), *Communications between Doctors and Patients.* London: Nuffield Provincial Hospitals Trust.

Ley, P. (1977). Psychological studies of doctor–patient communication. In S. Rachman (ed.), *Contributions to Medical Psychology,* 1. Oxford: Pergamon.

Ley, P. (1978). Psychological and behavioural factors in weight loss. In G. A. Bray (ed.), *Recent Advances in Obesity Research,* 2. London: Newman Publishing.

Ley, P. (1979a). Improving communications: Effects of altering doctor behaviour. In D. J. Oborne, M. M. Gruneberg & J.R. Eiser (eds), *Research in Psychology and Medicine.* London: Academic Press.

Ley, P. (1979b). The psychology of compliance. In D. J. Oborne, M. M. Gruneberg & J. R. Eiser (eds), *Research in Psychology and Medicine,* Vol. 2. London: Academic Press.

Ley, P. (1979c). Memory for medical information. *British Journal of Social and Clinical Psychology,* **18**, 245–256.

Ley, P. (1980a). The psychology of obesity. In S. Rachman (ed.) *Contributions to Medical Psychology,* 2. Oxford: Pergamon.

Ley, P. (1980b). Practical methods for improving communication. In L. Morris, M. Mazis, & L. Barofsky (eds), *Product Labelling and Health Risks.* Cold Spring Harbour, NY: Banbury Reports.

Ley, P. (1981). Professional non-compliance: A neglected problem. *British Journal of Clinical Psychology,* **20**, 151–154.

Ley, P. (1982a). Giving information to patients. In J. R. Eiser (ed.), *Social Psychology and Behavioural Medicine.* New York: Wiley.

Ley, P. (1982b). Simplification, adjunct questions and the recall of ophthalmological and pediatric information leaflets. (in press).

Ley, P. & Spelman, M. S. (1965). Communications in an out-patient setting. *British Journal of Social and Clinical Psychology,* **4**, 114–116.

Ley, P. & Spelman, M. S. (1967). *Communicating with the Patient.* London: Staples Press.

Ley, P. & Goldman, M., Bradshaw, P. W., Kincey, J. A. & Walker, C. (1972). The comprehensibility of some x-ray leaflets. *Journal of the Insititute of Health Education,* **10**, 47–53.

Ley, P., Bradshaw, P. W., Eaves, D. & Walker, C. M. (1973). A method for increasing patients recall of information presented by doctors. *Psychological Medicine.* **3**, 217–220.

Ley, P., Bradshaw, P. W., Kincey, J. A. Couper-Smartt, J. & Wilson, M. (1974). Psychological variables in the control of obesity. In W. Burland, P. D. Samuel & J. Yudkin (eds), *Obesity.* London: Churchill-Livingstone.

Ley, P., Bradshaw, P. W. Kincey, J.A. & Atherton, S. T. (1976a). Increasing patients satisfaction with communications. *British Journal of Social and Clinical Psychology,* **15**, 403–413.

Ley, P. Whitworth, M. A., Skilbeck, C. E., Woodward, R., Pinsent, R.J.F.H., Pike, L. A., Clarkson, M. E. & Clark, P. B. (1976b). Improving doctor–patient communication in general practice. *Journal of the Royal College of General Practitioners,* **26**, 720–724.

Ley, P., Pike, L. A., Whitworth, M . A. & Woodward, R. (1979). Effects of source, context of communication and difficulty level on the success of health education and communications. *Health Education Journal,* **38**, 47–52.

Liguori, S. (1978). A quantitative assessment of the readability of PPIs. *Drug Intelligence and Clinical Pharmacy,* **12**, 712–716.

McGuire, W. J. (1980). The communication-persuasion model and health risk labelling. In L. A. Morris, M. B. Mazis, & I. Barofsky (eds), *Banbury Report 6. Product Labelling and Health Risks.* Cold Spring Harbor, NY: Cold Spring Harbor Laboratories.

Maguire, P. (1979). Teaching essential interviewing skills to medical students. In D. Oborne, M. M. Gruneberg & J. R. Eiser (eds), *Research in Psychology and Medicine.* London: Academic Press.

Maguire, P. & Rutter, D. R. (1976). Training medical students to communicate. In A. E. Bennett (ed.), *Communication between Doctors and Patients.* London: Oxford University Press for the Nuffield Provincial Hospitals Trust.

Mangelsdorff, A. D. (1979). Patient satisfaction questionnaire. *Medical Care,* **17**, 86–90.

Morris, L. A. & Halperin, J. (1979). Effects of written drug information on patient knowledge and compliance: A literature review. *American Journal of Public Health,* **69**, 47–52.

Myers, E. D. & Calvert, E. J. (1973). Effects of forewarning on the occurrence of side-effects and discontinuance of medication in patients on amitryptiline. *British Journal of Psychiatry,* **122**, 461–464.

Myers, E. D. & Calvert, E. J. (1976). Effect of forewarning on the occurrence of side-effects and discontinuance of medication in patients on dothiepen. *Journal of International Medical Research,* **4**, 237–240.

Myers, E. D. & Calvert, E. J. (1978). Knowledge of side effects and perseverance with medication. *British Journal of Psychiatry,* **132**, 526–527.

Ostwalt, R. M. (1979). A review of the experimental manipulation of blood donor motivation. In D. Oborne, M. M. Gruneberg & J. R. Eiser (eds), *Research in Psychology and Medicine.* London: Academic Press.

Pendleton, D. (1979). Assessing the communication difficulty in general practice consultations. In D. Oborne, M. M. Gruneberg & J. R. Eiser (eds), *Research in Psychology and Medicine.* London: Academic Press.

Priluck, I. A., Robertson, D. M. & Buettner, H. (1979). What patients recall of the preoperative discussion after retinal detachment surgery. *American Journal of Ophthalmology,* **87**, 620–623.

Pyrczak, F. & Roth, D. M. (1976). The readability of directions on non-prescription drugs. *Journal of the American Pharmaceutical Association,* **16**, 242–243, 267.

Raphael, W. & Peers, V. (1972). *Psychiatric Patients View their Hospitals.* London: King Edward's Hospital Fund.

Robinson, G. & Merav, A. (1976). Informed consent: Recall by patients tested post-operatively. *Annals of Thoracic Surgery,* **22**, 209–212.

Roghmann, K. J., Hengst, A. H. & Zastowny, T. R. (1979). Satisfaction with medical care. *Medical Care,* **17**, 461–477.

Roter, D. (1977). Patient participation in the patient–provider interaction. *Health Education Monographs,* **5**, 281–315.

Roter, D. (1979). Altering patient behaviour in interaction with providers. In D. J. Oborne, M. M. Gruneberg & J. R. Eiser (eds), *Research in Psychology and Medicine*, vol. 2. London: Academic Press.

Roth, H. P. (1979). Problems in conducting a study of the effects on patient compliance of teaching the rationale for antacid therapy. In S. J. Cohen (ed.), *New Directions in Patient Compliance.* Lexington, MA: Lexington Books.

Rutter, D. R. & Maguire, G. (1976). History taking for medical students II. Evaluation of a training programme. *Lancet,* **i**, 558–560.

Sackett, D. L. & Haynes, R. B. (1976). *Compliance with Therapeutic Regimens.* Baltimore: Johns Hopkins University Press.

Sackett, D. L., Haynes, R. B., Gibson, E., Sackett, B. C., Taylor, D. W., Roberts, R. S. & Johnson, A. L. (1975). Randomized clinical trial of strategies for improving medication compliance in primary hypertension. *Lancet,* **i**, 1205–1207.

Skilbeck, C. E., Tulips, J. G., J. G. & Ley, P. (1977). The effects of fear arousal, fear position, fear exposure, and sidedness on compliance with dietary instructions. *European Journal of Social Psychology,* **7**, 221–239.

Stevens, D. P., Stagg, R. N. & Mackay, I. R. (1977). What happens when hospitalised patients see their records. *Annals of Internal Medicine,* **86**, 474–477.

Stimson, G. W. (1974). Obeying doctors orders: A view from the other side. *Social Science and Medicine,* **8**, 97–104.

Ware, J. E. & Snyder, M. K. (1975). Dimensions of patient attitudes regarding doctors and medical care services. *Medical Care,* **13**, 669–682.

Received 22 February 1982

Requests for reprints should be addressed to Philip Ley, Department of Psychology, University of Sydney, NSW 2006, Australia.

Recognition of patients' worries by nurses and by other patients

Marie Johnston

Previous studies indicate that patients' worries may not be communicated very effectively to hospital staff. The current study examines whether other patients know more about surgical patients' worries than the nursing staff on the ward. For each patient, the patient, a nurse and a colleague-patient completed a checklist to describe the patients' worries. The results showed that the other patients were more accurate than the nurses both in terms of overall accuracy and, more tentatively, using signal detection theory estimates of sensitivity. As in a previous study, the nurses overestimated the number of worries; the overestimation did not appear to be related to the content of the items nor was it due to patients' underreporting of problems. Relationships between patients, both on the surgical ward and in self-help groups, are discussed.

Do patients reveal their worries more accurately to nurses or to other patients? The literature on satisfaction with hospital communication (Ley, 1976) suggests that one of the reasons for poor communications is patient diffidence about interrupting the activities of apparently busy staff, which may result in their main concerns remaining unvoiced. Alternatively, the patients may discuss their worries with other patients with whom they are in constant contact and who are clearly less busy. This informal hospital network is generally recognized, but has not been studied in any detail.

There is evidence that patients fail to communicate their worries to staff. Johnston (1976) asked surgical patients to complete the Hospital Adjustment Inventory (HAI) (De Wolfe *et al.*, 1966) to describe their worries and simultaneously a nurse filled in a similar form for each patient to indicate how much she knew of the patient's worries. The results indicated poor concordance between nurse and patient, suggesting that nurses had very limited information about patients' concerns.

In a rather different setting, a paediatric clinic, Korsch & Negrete (1972) found that the single most common criticism of doctors by the mothers was that they failed to deal with her main concerns. Given that this study also found a relationship between patient satisfaction and compliance with medical advice, it may be important to elicit these concerns, and the results suggest that the doctors may often fail to identify the mother's worries.

If doctors and nurses do not know what the individual patient is worrying about, then they are unlikely to be able to reassure the patient and give information relevant to his or her worries. Previous research (Johnston, 1980) indicates that surgical patients have continuing high levels of anxiety for long periods following surgery and certainly continuing after the life-threatening or painful medical procedures have been completed. This may reflect on inability of the staff to give the patient appropriate information and reassurance. In the study of nurse–patient communication mentioned above (Johnston, 1976) nurses were not only inaccurate, but showed a strong response bias, identifying almost three times as many worries as the patient reported. Nurses might then be giving copious amounts of inappropriate reassurance.

There is now a large literature on giving preparatory communication to surgical patients (e.g. see Ley, 1977). Some of the communications are designed to give the information and reassurance which is omitted under the normal ward routine. While the inputs vary greatly and the results also tend to be rather mixed, it is clear that patients' post-operative emotional state and recovery can benefit from such communications. The components of successful pre-operative communications have not been identified and there may be several

0144-6657/82/040255 – 07 $02.00/0 © 1982 The British Psychological Society

unpublished studies, such as Staite (1978), where no effect is found. The critical factor may be the match between the information etc. contained in the communication and the unresolved worries of the patients in the particular setting; failure to detect patients' worries accurately would then lead to non-significant results. If so, teaching strategies of coping (e.g. Langer *et al.*, 1974) might be a more successful general principle as it does not depend on identifying individual worries.

Studies which have looked at hospital patients' worries (e.g. Volicer & Bohannon, 1975; Johnston 1976; Wilson-Barnett, 1976) have not necessarily identified the most obvious ranking of worries. For example, Volicer finds that having to eat cold or tasteless food is more stressful than thinking one might have pain because of surgery or test procedures. The study to be reported attempts to examine whether the ignorance of patients' worries demonstrated by Johnston (1976) is confined to nurses or whether it is also true of their fellow-patients; because of their close proximity, their ample opportunity to discuss their worries and the kind of role relationships that develop on a surgical ward, patients may have knowledge about each other that is denied to the staff. This was examined by replicating the study of Johnston (1976) with a fellow-patient as well as a nurse informant.

Since the previous study of nurse – patient communication revealed evidence of response bias in nurses, the analysis cannot simply deal with the number of accurately identified worries. Nurses might appear sensitive to their patients' worries by endorsing every item, but this would be achieved at the expense of many 'false positives' and would reflect response bias rather than sensitivity. Signal detection theory analyses were used in an attempt to measure sensitivity independently of this bias.

Method

Subjects

(*a*) The *patients* were 20 female in-patients all on one ward and aged between 24 and 65 years, who had had gynaecological surgery on average five days previously (range 2 – 9 days). Eleven women had had hysterectomies, the remainder having various types of surgical repair, cystectomy, oopherectomy and salpingectomy.

(*b*) *Nurses* were identified by each patient as the nurse currently on duty with whom she had had most contact. A total of 17 nurses were involved, three nurses each reporting on two patients. Three of the nurses were still in training.

Materials

The Hospital Adjustment Inventory (HAI) (De Wolfe *et al.*, 1966) was used as in the previous study (Johnston, 1976). It contains 22 items each asking about the presence or absence of a different worry, requiring the subject to circle 'yes' or 'no' respectively.

Procedure

The questionnaires were administered by a research worker who went to the ward at intermittent intervals to avoid any systematic bias which might result from regular visits. Women who were fit to complete questionnaires were identified and asked to complete the HAI. Each was then asked to name the patient and the nurse currently on duty with whom she had most contact. The named individuals were then asked to complete the HAI as soon as possible to describe how the patient felt. They were told that it was a study of the extent to which patrients revealed their feelings and that the patient was completing a similar form to describe her own current feelings. The research worker ensured that there was no contact between the patient and the other two (the patient's colleague and her nurse) before the forms were completed.

The identification of the patient colleague (C) and the nurse (N) ensured that the research was tapping the most likely communication routes and that the respondents were participating in a meaningful task. Colleagues were identified in such a way that 10 mutually selected pairs of patients entered the study, giving some validity to the selection process involved. Thus each patient responded both for herself and for her colleague and will be identified either as Patient (P) or Colleague (C) according to the role taken.

The study was restricted to one ward and to a small number of patients because of its limited acceptability to nursing staff.

Analysis

The results allow comparison between each P, C, and N trio in the total worries identified, the total number of worries correctly identified and the type of item producing errors. (Throughout the analysis, the P response is taken as the 'correct' response, but this issue will be discussed later.)

In addition, an analysis which takes account of response bias was also included, using single point estimates of the area under the ROC (receiver operating characteristic) curve, P ($\overline{A}$), as an estimate of sensitivity for each C and N. By graphing hit and false-alarm rates for each C and N it is also possible to identify the more sensitive reporter for each patient and, by using a sign test, compare the sensitivity of C and N. These methods are described in more detail by McNicol (1972).

Results

Total worries

Patients on average endorsed $3 \cdot 9 \pm 3 \cdot 23$ worries (range 0 to 12) similar to the figure ($3 \cdot 41$) found previously (Johnston, 1976). The average for C and N were $4 \cdot 8 \pm 4 \cdot 11$ and $7 \cdot 75 \pm 3 \cdot 08$ respectively. These scores are shown in Fig. 1.

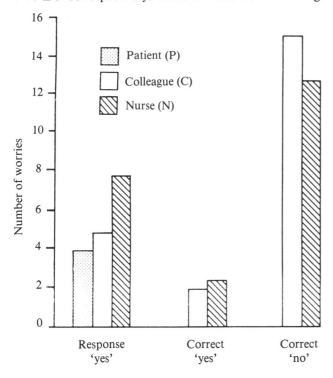

Figure 1. Total worries and correct responses.

The N scores were higher than the P scores for 18 patients and lower for two. The N scores were higher than C scores for 13 patients and lower for four. Thus the N scores were significantly higher than P or C scores ($P<0 \cdot 01$ for both comparisons, Wilcoxon's test for pair differences). In the previous study, nurses also overestimated patients' worries, in 88 per cent of cases.

There was no significant difference between P and C scores, P being greater in six cases, C in 10 cases ($P>0 \cdot 1$, Wilcoxon's test for pair differences). The rank order correlation between total scores for P and C was $0 \cdot 32$, not significant, and for P and N was $0 \cdot 46$,

$P<0\cdot05$. Thus the nurses showed some success in identifying the relative number of worries of patients although patients' colleagues did not.

The similarity in the behaviour of each patient when acting as P and acting as C was explored firstly by correlating total scores under the two conditions. The rank order correlation was $0\cdot77$, $P<0\cdot01$. In addition the number of items endorsed by the patient both as P and as C was calculated. On average, $2\cdot4$ items were checked both as C and as P, $2\cdot4$ items were checked as C but not as P, and $1\cdot5$ items were checked as P but not as C.

Accuracy

Colleagues (C) identified 49 per cent of patients' worries while N identified 59 per cent. On the other hand, C correctly identified the absence of worry on 84 per cent of occasions, N on 70 per cent (see Fig. 1). Figure 2 shows the percentage of correct responses given by C plotted against the percentage of correct responses by N for each patient. Both C and N score above the chance level of 50 per cent for most patients. The diagonal line indicates equal accuracy by C and N which was found for three patients. In three cases the N achieve more correct responses and for the remaining 14, C are more accurate. Thus C are significantly more accurate than N ($P<0\cdot02$, Wilcoxon's test for pair differences).

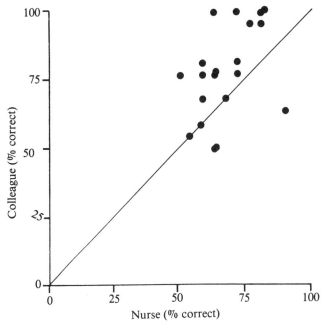

Figure 2. Percentage of correct responses (yes and no) by colleague (C) and nurse (N) for each patient.

Since patients may achieve accuracy when responding as C by replicating their P responses, the accuracy achieved on the $2\cdot4$ C items which were identical to the patients' own P items was compared with the accuracy on the $2\cdot4$ C items which were not checked as P items. The accuracy rate was identical, $1\cdot0$ items in each case.

Given that N scores overestimate the worries, their success rate is achieved at great cost — their false positive rate being 70 per cent, but the C rate of 60 per cent is also high. A clearer analysis of the relative sensitivity of C and N is obtained by signal detection theory parameters. A measure of sensitivity, P (Ā), was calculated for each C and N. C showed higher sensitivity than N in 14 pairs and was lower in four pairs; Wilcoxon's test for pair differences indicates that P (Ā) is significantly higher for C than N ($P = 0\cdot05$) indicating greater sensitivity of colleagues than nurses.

Since there may be a tendancy to underestimate P (Ā) in data with response bias (McNicol, 1972), C and N scores were also compared for each patient by the graphing method which is not subject to such bias and is described by McNicol (1972, pp. 31–40). When this analysis was applied to all 20 patients, 13 comparisons fell in the uncertain areas, six showed greater sensitivity of C scores and one showed greater sensitivity of N score. While the tendency is for C to give more sensitive responses than N, the high proportion of uncertain comparisons makes this analysis of limited value for these data.

Items

The frequency of endorsement of each item is shown in Table 1. In order to explore the nature of the nurse's overestimations, the discrepancy between the number of N and P endorsements was calculated and the items arranged from those most frequently overestimated to those most frequently underestimated by nurses.

Table 1. Analysis of item overestimation by nurses

Item no.	Brief description	Discrepancy between totals		Number of correct responses		Number of patients answering 'Yes'
		N & P	C & P	N	C	
3	When will get out of hospital	12	5	6	11	6
6	Not having enough to do on ward	10	0	10	20	0
11	Making enough progress in recovery	8	−1	10	11	10
5	Noise/confusion on ward	6	3	13	15	2
22	Children cared for properly	6	2	12	14	2
13	Getting adequate medical help	6	5	12	15	1
20	Keeping up payments on home/car	5	1	15	19	0
14	Will be as strong as before	4	−1	14	11	9
4	Associate closely with people on ward	4	2	14	18	0
2	Get pension or compensation	4	1	16	19	0
21	Possible illness in family	3	0	5	12	9
19	Will get a job when get out	3	0	15	18	1
1	How to pay bills while in hospital	3	1	17	19	0
17	Lack of sex life	3	1	17	19	0
12	Will be able to hold down a job again	2	−1	13	15	4
18	Will be accepted by people after	1	1	19	19	0
16	Husband may walk out while in hospital	1	0	19	20	0
10	Being transferred to another ward/hospital	0	0	12	10	11
8	Visitors will come	0	−3	12	12	9
9	Whether doctors/nurses like you	−1	−2	11	14	8
7	To be so confined	−1	4	15	14	4
15	Might catch disease from patients on ward	−2	0	18	16	2

Nurses were most likely to overestimate worries about discharge, occupation and progress, items on which they showed low accuracy, and to underestimate worries about catching disease, being confined and being liked by staff.

Table 1 also shows the discrepancy between total C and P scores for each item. Items overestimated by N are not consistently overestimated by C. Both C and N show highest overestimation on worry about discharge.

The rank order correlations over 22 items between the number of Ps endorsing each item and the number of Cs and Ns endorsing each item were 0·90 and 0·70 respectively. In both cases, there is significant agreement about which items are more likely to be worrying.

Discussion

The results show that other patients are more accurate in estimating the number of worries a patient has and tend to be more sensitive in detecting which worries a patient has than are nurses with responsibility for the patient. Nurses overestimate the number of worries the patient has with the result that they have a high number of false positives, and therefore reduced sensitivity and lower overall accuracy.

These results confirm the findings of the previous study that nurses are not particularly good at identifying the worries of an individual patient. The high false positive rate is likely to result in nurses dealing with worries that patients do not have and, as a result, being inefficient at reassuring where relevant.

Other patients do not overestimate patients' worries and appear to be more sensitive to the individual patient's worries. The patients endorse a similar number of items when acting in the role of P and of C and some of the success of colleagues might be due to each patient describing her colleague to be like herself. Half of the worries attributed to the other patient were worries which the patient described herself as having, the remaining half being separate worries. However, this cannot explain the extra success of patients as their accuracy rate was equal on both shared and unshared items.

Patients may not only describe their colleagues as having a similar number of worries, they may also actually be like their colleagues, the similarity being due both to the selection procedure adopted and to social influences on the ward. While the numbers are rather small for valid statistical analysis, the rank order correlation between the self-report scores of patients and colleagues does approach significance ($0 \cdot 48$). The patients may therefore achieve some success by being similar. Alternatively, the communication may be facilitated by the increased opportunity in terms of time spent together, often in close proximity, and the greater equality of status and role in their relationship.

If other patients have this understanding of the patient's worries, they may be in a position to help reduce the worries. Studies in which preparatory communications for surgery are done in groups (e.g. Lindeman, 1972; Schmitt & Wooldrige, 1973) may capitalize on this, and in other fields the benefits of using self-help groups or peer therapists are being recognized. For example, the numerous voluntary organisations such as the Schizophrenia Fellowship, U & I, Alcoholics Anonymous, the Phobics Society, suggest that fellow-sufferers may provide some comfort, information, etc., which is not available elsewhere. Recent evidence in the treatment of agoraphobia suggests that spouses may function as very successful therapists (Mathews *et al.*, 1977) perhaps because, like the patients' colleagues in a surgical ward, they have the time, the relationship and sufficient identification to be responsive to the patients' concerns.

The nurses' overestimation of patients' worries may be open to alternative interpretations as it rests on the assumption that the patient's report is the 'true' estimate. Nurses also overestimated patients' worries in the previous study (Johnston, 1976) and it might be argued that this reflects not an inaccuracy by the nurses, but underreporting by the patients. For example, patients might see the task as reporting only worries that exceeded their expectations or the perceived norm on the ward. However, in the previous study, there was evidence that the nurses underestimated patients' physical distress as assessed by the Recovery Inventory, including pain measures, and therefore the data do not indicate a general tendency by patients to underreport distress. One would have to postulate that patients were more reticent about reporting worries than physical distress; nurses might know of concerns which the patient was unwilling to admit on the questionnaire as a result of a social desirability bias. Examination of the data in Table 1 suggests that the largest discrepancies between nurse and patient occur on items that are unlikely to lead to such a bias. Also, there is no evidence that the patients overestimate the same items as the nurses when they report as colleagues and might be less constrained by social desirability. The size of the discrepancy between nurses and patients appears unrelated to frequency of patient endorsement and unrelated to the relevance of the item to the nurse's tasks; for example, an equal number of nurses and patients endorsed the item on transfer but 12 more nurses than patients endorsed the item on discharge. Thus nurses are not simply exaggerating unusual worries or making wild guesses about worries that might not be considered appropriate for discussion between the nurse and her patient, such as concerns about events at home.

Nurses achieved some success in rank ordering patients by number of worries, the previous study having shown a non-significant correlation. This suggests that the nurses in the current study might be able to identify the most worried patients but would not know what they worried about and would tend to overestimate the number of worries. If so, then they might at least know which patients are most likely to need reassuring. However, this is a weak finding, not obtained in the previous study. Patients' colleagues do not manage to rank order patients according to their number of worries.

Both patients and colleagues, and patients and nurses achieved a high degree of agreement about which items were likely to be worrying. In addition, the items most frequently endorsed in this study were those most frequently endorsed in the previous study and similarly for the least frequently endorsed items. There would appear to be considerable agreement about *what* is worrying compared with the poorer agreement about *who* is worrying.

The signal detection theory analysis used in this study is reported tentatively due to reservations noted in the results section. With more development of the methods involved, this type of analysis might allow one to comment on communication as the simple transmission of a message between a patient and a doctor or vice versa, without including the much more complex behaviour involved in memory, compliance and satisfaction which have been the more usual measures of communication efficiency (Ley, 1977).

Acknowledgements

I wish to thank the nurses and patients of the Churchill Hospital, Oxford, and members of the Health Services Evaluation Group for their contributions to this study. The work was partly supported by a DHSS grant.

References

Bennett, A. E. (ed.) (1976). *Communications Between Doctors and Patients.* London: Nuffield Provincial Hospitals Trust.
DeWolfe, A. S., Barrell, R. P. & Cummings, J. W. (1966). Patient variables in emotional responses to hospitalization for physical illness. *Journal of Consulting Psychology,* 30, 68–72.
Johnston, M. (1976). Communication of patients' feelings in hospital. In Bennett (1976).
Johnston, M. (1980). Anxiety in surgical patients. *Psychological Medicine,* 10, 145–152.
Korsch, B. M. & Negrete, V. F. (1972). Doctor-patient communication. *Scientific American,* August, 66–73.
Langer, E. S. Janis, I. L. & Wolfer, J. A. (1974). Reduction of psychological stress in surgical patients. *Journal of Experimental Social Psychology,* 11, 155–165.
Ley, P. (1976). Toward better doctor–patient communications. Contributions from social and experimental psychology. In Bennett (1976).
Ley, P. (1977). Psychological studies of doctor–patient communication. In S. Rachman (ed.), *Contributions to Medical Psychology,* vol. 1. Oxford: Pergamon.
Lindeman, C. A. (1972). Nursing intervention with the pre-surgical patient. *Nursing Research,* 21, 196–209.
Mathews, A., Teasdale, J., Munby, M., Johnston, D. & Shaw, P. (1977). A home-based treatment programme for agoraphobia. *Behavior Therapy,* 8, 915–924.
McNicol, C. A. (1972). *A Primer of Signal Detection Theory.* London: Allen & Unwin.
Schmitt, F. E. & Wooldridge, P. J. (1973). Psychological preparation of surgical patients. *Nursing Research,* 22, 108–116.
Staite, S. (1978). The effect of giving information about post-operative sensations on mood and pain in patients undergoing gynaecological surgery. Unpublished MPhil Thesis, University of London.
Volicer, B. J. & Bohannon, M. W. (1975). A Hospital Stress Rating Scale. *Nursing Research,* 24, 352–359.
Wilson-Barnett, J. (1976). Patients' emotional reactions to hospitalization: An exploratory study. *Journal of Advanced Nursing,* 1, 351–358.

Received 15 March 1982

Requests for reprints should be addressed to Dr M. Johnston, Academic Department of Psychiatry, Royal Free Hospital, Pond Street, London NW3 2QG, UK.

British Journal of Clinical Psychology (1982), **21**, 263 – 269 *Printed in Great Britain*

Perceived control and the experience of childbirth

Chris Brewin and **Clare Bradley***

This study investigated the relationship between women's expectations of control during labour and the experience of childbirth. The women's expectations about their personal ability and about the ability of the staff to exercise control over, labour were examined. It was predicted that women who attended childbirth preparation classes would be less anxious about, and anticipate more control over, labour than non-attenders. Among the attenders, perceived personal control was expected to be related to self-reports of a more satisfying and less painful birth, while among the non-attenders beneficial effects were expected to be associated with greater perceived staff control. It was found that class attendance was associated with enhanced perception of personal and staff control but not with decreased anxiety. Class attendance and perceptions of personal and staff control predicted less painful (but not more satisfying) labour. A multiple regression analysis indicated that in the sample as a whole, perception of staff control was the single best predictor of reported discomfort. As expected, this was not equally true of attenders and non-attenders. Perceived staff control was a better predictor of reported discomfort in non-attenders while among class attenders perceptions of personal control were closely associated with the later reported experience of discomfort.

Numerous claims have been made for the benefits of psychoprophylactic preparation for childbirth, but until recently there has been little reliable research evidence (Beck & Hall, 1978). More carefully controlled studies have supported some of these claims, principally for the effects of preparation on self-report variables such as ratings of pain or satisfaction. Charles *et al.* (1978) reported that prepared subjects rated their experience of labour as less painful and more enjoyable, a result that could not be attributed to the confounding effects of age, socio-economic status or parity. The prepared subjects also tended to receive lower levels of analgesia and anaesthesia, but in these cases the possible influence of their relatively greater age and social status was not evaluated. There appeared to be no effects of preparation on other obstetric variables. Beck *et al.* (1980) also found that prior preparation predicted pain ratings but not other obstetric variables.

In order to improve psychoprophylactic preparation for childbirth, the psychological variables which mediate its effects should now be investigated. Two possible variables are the woman's level of anxiety prior to labour and her perception of control over the process of labour. The evidence for the mediating effects of anxiety is, however, very mixed. Gorsuch & Key (1974), for instance, found that state anxiety in the first three months was related to abnormalities of pregnancy and delivery but measures of anxiety taken later were not so related. Lederman *et al.* (1978) suggested that anxiety might tend to prolong labour owing to the action of adrenalin secretion on uterine contractile activity. In their study, they found that state anxiety at the onset of stage 2 labour correlated with the level of endogenous plasma adrenalin, which in turn correlated with the duration of labour, but there was no direct relationship between anxiety and length of labour. In contrast, Beck *et al.* (1980) reported that higher anxiety on entering the labour ward was followed by a relatively shorter labour. In this study, anxiety was not found to be related to the use of anaesthesia or analgesia or to the incidence of obstetric complications. One of the few studies to report widespread effects of anxiety was that of Crandon (1979 *a, b*) who found that anxiety in the last three months of pregnancy was predictive of a wide range of

---

*Order of authorship was determined by the toss of a coin.

0144-6657/82/040263 – 07 $02.00/0 © 1982 The British Psychological Society

obstetric abnormalities, including either prolonged or precipitate labour and lower foetal Apgar scores. It is not clear, however, whether these results might be accounted for by age, parity, or other variables which may differ between women with high and low anxiety.

There are indications in the psychological literature that perception of control over a painful stimulus may lead to greater tolerance of pain (Bowers, 1968). In addition, perceived control appears to reduce the extent of physiological change associated with stressful experiences (Geer *et al.*, 1970; Glass & Singer, 1972). It therefore seems likely that psychoprophylaxis may be effective because it increases the sense of competence or mastery with which a woman approaches childbirth. The only evidence pertinent to this hypothesis comes from a study by Scott-Palmer & Skevington (1981), who correlated women's self-reports of pain with their internal – external locus of control orientation. They found that women with an external locus of control (women who in general believed that they had relatively less control over the environment) tended to have longer periods of labour but to report less pain than women with an internal locus of control. This study poses a number of interesting questions. First, did the general measure of locus of control reflect the women's specific feelings of control over the process of childbirth? How many of the women had attended childbirth preparation classes? Was this decision related to their locus of control scores? Finally, were the results attributable to differential use of medication by women with internal and women with external loci of control? The study raises the additional possibility that there may be a group of women with an internal locus of control who prefer to have more personal control over labour and there may also be a group of women with an external locus of control who prefer to perceive the staff as having control.

The present study was designed to examine these issues. Women were interviewed shortly before giving birth. At the interview, their anxiety about giving birth was measured, together with the degree of control which they themselves and the medical staff were expected to exercise over the length and discomfort of labour. In this context, personal control might mean one of two things: the woman might feel able to manage the experience either through her own personal resources or through directing the staff to satisfy her requirements. The present study was concerned with the measurement of personal control in the first sense, primarily through the use of psychoprophylactic breathing and relaxation techniques.

It was predicted that women who had attended classes would feel less anxious about giving birth, but in view of the conflicting findings reported elsewhere, no prediction was made concerning the effects of anxiety on labour variables. Class attenders were also expected to feel more able to control the length and discomfort of labour. Furthermore, for women who had attended classes, it was expected that perceptions of personal control would correlate positively with reported satisfaction and negatively with reported discomfort. For non-attenders, perceptions of control by staff were expected to correlate positively with reported satisfaction and negatively with reported discomfort.

Method

Subjects

Women attending the antenatal clinic of a large general hospital and in their 39th week of pregnancy were invited to take part in a study investigating the relationship between expectations of childbirth and subsequent experience of labour and delivery. Subjects were white, indigenous English-speaking women for whom no obstetric complications were expected. Because of the shortage of primigravidae who had not attended childbirth preparation classes, the duration of the study was extended to allow an extra five women, all fulfilling the above selection criteria, to be recruited. Out of a total sample of 78, three women refused to participate in the study. The mean age of the sample was 25·6 years (range 15 – 43 years), and it included 10 single and 68 married women. The hospital served a predominantly working-class area. Sixty of the women had finished full-time education by age 16. Forty-four were having their first baby and 34 a second or subsequent baby. Fifty of the women had been to childbirth preparation classes, 42 of them during the current pregnancy. These classes included instruction in psychoprophylaxis and information about childbirth and baby care. Women were classed as attenders only if they had been to a minimum of five classes, a restriction which excluded a further seven women. There were 28 women who had not attended any preparation classes.

Measures and procedure

At the initial interview, women answered the following questions on seven-point Likert scales: (*a*) How anxious are you about giving birth? (not anxious at all − extremely anxious); (*b*) How worried are you about experiencing discomfort during labour? (not worried at all − extremely worried); (*c*) To what extent do you think you will actually be able to help to make your baby arrive more quickly during labour? (cannot help at all − can help a great deal); (*d*) To what extent do you think you will actually be able to help to reduce discomfort during labour? (cannot help at all − can help a great deal); (*e*) To what extent do you think the nurses and doctors can help to make your baby arrive more quickly? (cannot help at all − can help a great deal); (*f*) To what extent do you think the nurses and doctors can help to reduce discomfort during labour? (cannot help at all − can help a great deal). In answering the personal control items (*c* and *d*), a few women initially understood the items to refer to their expectations of being able to control staff behaviour. On these occasions it was necessary to explain that the items were intended to refer to control through the women's own personal resources.

In each case, immediately after delivery, the midwife completed a questionnaire giving details of the length of labour, use of anaesthesia and analgesia, the occurrence of any obstetric complications, and the 1-minute and 5-minute Apgar scores of the baby. On the following day, the subjects completed a second questionnaire on which they rated the amount of discomfort they had experienced and the degree of satisfaction about the birth, using five-point scales. Eleven subjects failed to return the second questionnaire.

Results

It was expected that class attendance would be associated with increased expectations of personal control and with less anxiety about the birth. Table 1 shows the results of analyses of covariance on the pre-birth expectations, controlling for the influence of age, marital status, level of education, and parity (when controlling for parity, women were divided into two groups, those having their first baby or a subsequent baby). Table 1 shows that class attenders did not feel any less anxious about the birth, but perceived that they had more personal control over the discomfort they would experience ($F = 14 \cdot 97$, d.f. $= 1,64$, $P < 0 \cdot 001$). They also perceived more control over the duration of labour ($F = 4 \cdot 52$, d.f. $= 1,64$, $P < 0 \cdot 04$). Attenders also perceived staff as having more control over the discomfort they would experience ($F = 5 \cdot 33$, d.f. $= 1,64$, $P < 0 \cdot 03$).

Table 1. One-way analysis of covariance on pre-birth expectations: adjusted means and *F* values for class attenders and non-attenders (the covariates used were age, marital status, education and parity)

Class attendance	Anxiety		Personal control		Staff control	
	Giving birth	Discomfort	Duration	Discomfort	Duration	Discomfort
Attenders: means	3·79	3·30	4·41	4·93	5·76	6·43
Non-attenders: means	3·47	3·38	3·36	3·21	5·18	5·75
F (d.f. = 1,64)	0·30	0·02	4·52*	14·97**	1·72	5·33*

*$P < 0 \cdot 05$; **$P < 0 \cdot 001$.

Class attendance and ratings of anxiety and control were then correlated with the obstetric outcome variables and the self-reported experience of labour, once again controlling for the effects of age, marital status, education and parity. Neither class attendance nor the pre-birth ratings predicted satisfaction with the birth or any of the obstetric measures (which included use of anaesthesia and analgesia, length of labour, the

Table 2. Partial correlations of reported discomfort with class attendance and pre-birth expectations, controlling for age, marital status, education and parity (degrees of freedom in parentheses)

	Anxiety		Personal control		Staff control	
Class attendance	Giving birth	Discomfort	Duration	Discomfort	Duration	Discomfort
−0·33**	0·07	0·19	−0·28*	−0·20	−0·24*	−0·35**
(54)	(58)	(59)	(57)	(58)	(59)	(59)

*$P<0·05$; **$P<0·01$.

occurrence of complications and Apgar scores), with the following exceptions. Women who had felt more anxious about giving birth were more likely to have epidural anaesthesia ($r=0·27$, d.f. $=71$, $P<0·025$). Women who expected more personal control over the duration of labour were more likely to have their labour induced or accelerated pharmacologically ($r=0·32$, d.f. $=69$, $P<0·01$). The most consistent effects of class attendance and perceptions of control were the effects on reported discomfort. Table 2 shows that class attenders reported significantly less discomfort than non-attenders ($r=−0·33$, $P<0·01$). Anxiety was not significantly related to discomfort ratings, although there was a trend for those more anxious about discomfort to report more discomfort subsequently. Perceptions of control were, however, consistently related to discomfort, less pain being reported by women who had expected to have more personal control over the duration of labour ($r=−0·28$, $P<0·025$) and more personal control over discomfort ($r=−0·20$, $P<0·07$), and by women who had expected staff to have more control over the duration of labour ($r=−0·24$, $P<0·05$) and over their discomfort ($r=−0·35$, $P<0·005$). To check whether these relationships might be mediated by use of anaesthesia or analgesia, correlations were calculated between drug use and reported discomfort. Use of entonox and epidural anaesthesia were unrelated to reported discomfort while women who had used pethidine reported significantly more painful labours ($r=0·26$, d.f. $=65$, $P<0·05$). It therefore seems unlikely that class attenders and women with higher perceived control reported less discomfort simply because they made greater use of the available drugs.

Multiple regression analysis was next carried out to determine whether class attendance or perception of control made the greatest contribution to reported discomfort. The three variables showing the highest simple correlations with reported discomfort were entered into the equation together, so that the effects of each variable could be examined independently of the other two. The three variables together were significantly predictive of discomfort ($F=3·84$, d.f. $=3,56$, $P<0·05$). Table 3 shows that most of the variance was accounted for by the rating of perceived staff control over discomfort, the only variable to predict discomfort on its own ($F=5·36$, d.f. $=1,56$, $P<0·05$).

Table 3. Multiple regression with variables predicting self-reported discomfort

Variable	Simple r	Multiple r	Beta	F (d.f. $=1,56$)
Staff control: discomfort	−0·36	0·36	−0·30	5·36*
Class attendance	−0·19	0·38	0·05	0·16
Personal control: duration	−0·29	0·41	−0·18	1·83

*$P<0·05$.

Finally, the relationship of perception of control to reported discomfort was examined for class attenders and non-attenders separately. It was expected that perceptions of personal control would be related to discomfort in class attenders, whereas in non-attenders discomfort would be related to perceptions of staff control. Table 4 gives these partial correlations for the two groups of women, once again controlling for the effects of age, marital status, education and parity. The predictions appear to be borne out by two of the four measures, the other two failing to show any particular trend. Personal control over duration was significantly related to reported discomfort among attenders ($r = -0.41$, $P<0.01$) but not among non-attenders ($r=0.12$, n.s.). Attenders who anticipated personal control reported less discomfort during labour. In contrast, perceived staff control over discomfort was significantly related to reported discomfort among non-attenders ($r = -0.63$, $P<0.01$) but not among attenders ($r = -0.10$, n.s.). Non-attenders who perceived the staff to have control subsequently reported less discomfort. When the magnitude of the differences between these correlations was assessed, the relationship with personal control over duration was found to be significantly stronger in class attenders ($t=1.71$, $P<0.05$). Perceived staff control over discomfort was significantly more predictive of later reported discomfort among non-attenders ($t=1.97$, $P<0.01$).

Table 4. A comparison of intercorrelations between pre-birth expectations of control and reported discomfort in class attenders and non-attenders (degrees of freedom in parentheses)

Class attendance	Personal control		Staff control	
	Duration	Discomfort	Duration	Discomfort
Attenders	-0.41**	0.00	-0.17	-0.10
	(33)	(34)	(34)	(34)
Non-attenders	0.12	-0.27	0.37	-0.63**
	(14)	(14)	(14)	(14)
t (d.f. = 47)	1.71*	0.87	0.67	1.97**

*$P<0.05$; **$P<0.01$.

Discussion

Class attenders in this study were characterized by the belief that both they and the medical and nursing staff had greater control over the process of childbirth. They were not however any less anxious, a finding which echoes that of Astbury (1980) and may reflect the difficulty in distinguishing the adaptive and maladaptive functions of anxiety. The finding that attenders rated the staff as having more control also suggests that women who choose not to attend classes do not opt out because they have more confidence in the staff. Of course, it is not possible from this study to assess the impact of childbirth education on what may have been pre-existing differences between the two groups of women. Furthermore, it is not clear to what extent the present results may be generalized to other antenatal clinics, childbirth preparation classes and labour wards where there might be more or less opportunity to exercise personal control.

In common with other recent well-controlled studies (Charles *et al.*, 1978; Beck *et al.*, 1980), childbirth education and the psychological variables examined were not found to influence any obstetric variables. The only exceptions in the present study were that women who were more anxious or who perceived greater personal control were more likely to have epidural anaesthesia or pharmacological acceleration of labour respectively. Clearly, the potential impact of psychological variables will be limited by the amount of flexibility in the use of obstetric procedures in different hospitals and by the willingness of staff to be guided by the treatment preferences of each individual woman.

Psychological variables did however predict self-reported pain. Less pain was reported by class attenders and by women who perceived that either they themselves or the staff exercised greater control over labour. A multiple regression analysis on the data from the entire sample of women indicated that, of these three variables, the single most important for predicting reported discomfort was perception of staff control over discomfort. Women who had attended preparation classes had greater expectations of staff control than had the non-attenders. This would be expected given the nature of the classes which not only taught psychoprophylaxis but also provided information about the procedure in labour and the availability of medication. Hence, attenders would be likely to be more aware of the range of actions available to staff. However, it was the non-attenders who reported most discomfort in labour and it was the non-attenders for whom the relationship between perceptions of staff control and reported discomfort was particularly significant. The inference is that the non-attenders needed the information about pain-controlling medication which childbirth education can provide.

For class attenders, information about personal control may be correspondingly more important. It is possible that class attendance serves at least two distinct psychological functions, the first stage being one of changing beliefs about staff control and the second one of increasing perceptions of personal control. Alternatively, it may be that class attenders are characterized by greater initial confidence in medical and nursing staff and that classes primarily influence beliefs about personal control. Further research might profitably focus on two questions: (1) how might childbirth preparation classes influence the acquisition of beliefs about control, and (2) is it possible to make childbirth less painful for non-attenders by giving them extra information designed to reassure them and to enhance their perception of staff control?

Acknowledgements

The authors gratefully acknowledge Dr Sheila Duncan's help and advice in planning the study and for allowing access to her patients. The authors would also like to thank Anne Carling for her valuable assistance in interviewing and data processing and to thank the staff of the antenatal clinic, in particular Sister Winnard, and the midwives on the labour ward of the Northern General Hospital, Sheffield, and all the women who took part in the study.

References

Astbury, J. (1980). The crisis of childbirth: Can information and childbirth education help? *Journal of Psychosomatic Research,* **24,** 9–13.

Beck, N. C. & Hall, D. (1978). Natural childbirth: A review and analysis. *Obstetrics and Gynecology,* **52,** 371–379.

Beck, N. C., Siegel, L. J., Davidson, N. P., Kormeier, S., Breitenstein, A. & Hall, D. G. (1980). The prediction of pregnancy outcome: Maternal preparation, anxiety and attitudinal sets. *Journal of Psychosomatic Research,* **24,** 343–351.

Bowers, K. (1968). Pain, anxiety and perceived control. *Journal of Consulting and Clinical Psychology,* **32,** 596–602.

Charles, A. G., Norr, K. L., Block, C. R., Meyering, S. & Meyers, E. (1978). Obstetric and psychological effects of psychoprophylactic preparation for childbirth. *American Journal of Obstetrics and Gynecology,* **131,** 44–52.

Crandon, A. J. (1979*a*). Maternal anxiety and obstetric complications. *Journal of Psychosomatic Research,* **23,** 109–111.

Crandon, A. J. (1979*b*). Maternal anxiety and neonatal well-being. *Journal of Psychosomatic Research,* **23,** 113–115.

Geer, D. C., Davison, G. C. & Gatchel, R. J. (1970). Reduction of stress in humans through non-veridical perceived control of aversive stimulation. *Journal of Personality and Social Psychology,* **16,** 731–738.

Glass, D. C. & Singer, J. E. (1972). *Urban Stress: Experiments on Noise and Social Stressors.* New York: Academic Press.

Gorsuch, R. L. & Key, M. K. (1974). Abnormalities of pregnancy as a function of life stress. *Psychosomatic Medicine,* **36,** 352–362.

Lederman, R. P., Lederman, E., Work, B. A. & McCann, D. A. (1978). The relationship of maternal anxiety, plasma catecholamines, and plasma cortisol to progress in labour. *American Journal of Obstetrics and Gynecology,* **132,** 495–500.

Scott-Palmer, J. & Skevington, S. M. (1981). Pain during childbirth and menstruation: A study of locus of control. *Journal of Psychosomatic Research,* **25,** 151–155.

Received 24 February 1982

Requests for reprints should be addressed to Chris Brewin, Department of Psychiatry, University of Leeds, LS2 9LT, UK.

Clare Bradley is at the Department of Psychology, University of Sheffield.

British Journal of Clinical Psychology (1982), **21**, 271 – 280 *Printed in Great Britain*

Psychological preparation for surgery: A comparison of methods

Valerie Ridgeway and **Andrew Mathews**

Sixty hysterectomy patients were randomly assigned to one of three types of psychological preparation prior to surgery, while an additional 10 patients declined psychological help. Twenty patients received information about the surgical procedure and its effects, another 20 were instructed in a cognitive coping technique, and the remainder were given general information about the ward. Interventions were shown to have different effects on a number of pre- and post-surgical measures; notably on knowledge about hysterectomy, analgesic usage, reported days of pain after discharge, and belief in the usefulness of intervention methods. Whereas information about surgery enhanced knowledge and usefulness ratings, cognitive coping appeared to have most effect on indices of recovery. Patients declining preparation responded badly immediately after surgery, but made a satisfactory recovery after discharge. Cognitive coping methods seem to be an effective way of managing specific worries about the operation, and it is suggested that this underlies differences in patterns of recovery following surgery.

Patients having surgery are known to experience anxiety and uncertainty both before and after their operation (Wilson-Barnett, 1979; Johnston, 1980). Although it has long been assumed that pre-operative psychological state can affect physical recovery from surgery (e.g. Janis, 1958), only recently has more objective evidence emerged. Higher levels of neuroticism and trait anxiety for example, have been shown to correlate with poor physical recovery (Mathews & Ridgeway, 1981).

More convincing evidence of a causal relationship has been provided by the effectiveness of psychological preparation for surgery (see reviews by Auerbach & Kilman, 1977; Melamed, 1977; Kendall & Watson, 1981). With most interventions, hospitalized patients are seen a day or so before surgery, and are given information, instructions or reassurance, sometimes in combination (cf. Egbert *et al.,* 1964). Following surgery, selected indicators of recovery are evaluated such as subjective pain, analgesic consumption, physical complications and days in hospital. Despite some negative findings, the majority of studies have found prepared patients to have a better post-surgical recovery on one or more indices of recovery.

Types of intervention

The most common type of preparation involves giving the patient detailed information about the surgical procedure and its effects (e.g. Hayward, 1975). Examples of procedures typically covered would be the pre-medication injection, the surgical schedule, transfer to the recovery room, and the analgesic policy during recovery. The rationale for providing this information is that if the patient is surprised by procedures when they occur, then unnecessary worry could be provoked by what is actually quite normal. An example of this is provided by the reaction of patients to waking up with a routine intravenous drip in their arm, and interpreting this to mean something had gone wrong during the operation.

Alternatively, patients may be informed about actual sensations they are likely to experience, such as sleepiness, burning pain along the incision, dryness of mouth and so on. A certain amount of information about procedures is necessary to place the expected sensations in context. Also, a certain degree of reassurance is usually passed along in describing such sensations as normal. When sensation information has been compared with procedural information, the former was found to be more effective (Johnston, 1975) and it was suggested that congruency between expected and experienced sensations results in a lower emotional response.

0144-6657/82/040271 – 10 $02.00/0 © 1982 The British Psychological Society

In many of the reported studies, effects due to procedural or sensation information were confounded with instruction in behaviours known to enhance physical recovery (e.g. Egbert *et al.,* 1964; Hayward, 1975). These behaviours include breathing deeply, coughing, leg exercises, moving within and out of bed and ambulation. The reason for stressing such behaviours is that they help to avoid post-surgical complications, such as respiratory or circulation problems.

Other behavioural strategies showing considerable promise include practice in relaxation (Wilson, 1981) and the use of filmed modelling (Melamed, 1977). Modelling would appear to be a potent method of providing reassuring information, while relaxation may act by giving patients a means of controlling their own anxiety.

Two recent studies have employed explicit training in the use of cognitive coping methods directed at the patient's worries rather than providing information *per se* (Langer *et al.,* 1975, and Kendall *et al.,* 1979). Patients were asked to identify those aspects of surgery or hospitalization which concerned them, and were then encouraged to deal with these worries by viewing them in as positive a manner possible. Surgery may be likened to the events that are possible to appraise in a number of ways, and patients are helped to attend to the positive aspects of hospitalization, while countering any excessive and unfounded fears. In the only previous direct comparison of such cognitive coping methods with preparatory information prior to surgery, Langer *et al.* (1975) found the cognitive procedure to be superior in reducing medication requirements following surgery.

It would be particularly helpful to clinicians if those patients likely to profit from particular types of psychological intervention could be identified in advance. It might be that patients showing particular cognitive styles (for example, vigilance versus avoidance, or internal versus external locus of control) would respond in a systematically distinct manner to the giving or withholding of information. There are some indications that specific preparatory information may benefit vigilant more than avoidant patients, but interpretation is not helped by marked discrepancies between different studies (cf. Andrew, 1970; De Long, 1970). It is clear however that a certain (fairly small) proportion of patients disclaim the need for detailed information before surgery, and despite evidence that giving preparation across the board is not harmful (Wilson, 1981) it would not seem appropriate to force unwanted details on patients not wishing to receive them.

It is apparent even from this very brief review that a number of preparation methods may be effective, without it being obvious which method is best or which patients profit most. At present there does not seem any clear basis for assigning different types of patient to different preparatory methods, although our earlier review (Mathews & Ridgeway, 1981) suggests that patients with higher neuroticism or anxiety levels are more vulnerable in general. In studies where alternative anxiety reducing methods have been compared with standard information (Langer *et al.,* 1975; Kendall *et al.,* 1979; Wilson, 1981) the alternative methods appear to be as or more effective than information alone. Apart from clinical efficacy, the mechanism responsible for any effects of psychological preparation remains unclear. It has been suggested (Johnson, 1975) that information has its effect by minimizing the mismatch between expectation and experience; provided that a patient's experience is consistent with expectation then emotional reaction remains low. Thus, in common with alternative methods, the underlying mechanism is thought to be a reduction of anxiety, or other negative emotional response. If this is the case, then the different methods of preparation should be effective only to the extent that they reduce each patient's anxiety.

In the study to be reported here, women due for hysterectomy were randomly assigned to one of three types of preparation: information about the surgery and its effects, training in the use of a cognitive coping method, or general information about the ward. This last group was intended to control for the non-specific effects of attention and reassurance associated with the specific preparatory methods. By assessing the outcome of these three groups together with that of a further group who refused information it was hoped to determine the comparative effectiveness of the different methods, and to throw light on any interaction with personality or emotional response.

Method

All women admitted to St George's Hospital for elective abdominal hysterectomy between July 1980 and June 1981 were asked to participate in the study. Ten women were interviewed but declined further information, while the remaining 60 were randomly assigned to three types of preparation. An overview of the design and summary of the measures used is shown in Fig. 1.

Subjects

The seventy patients had a mean age of 42, ranging from 27 to 61. The majority were currently married (76 per cent), and had at least one child (84 per cent). Three-quarters were employed outside the home, and most were in social class two or three (79 per cent). All had a history of gynaecological problems that had not responded to previous medical treatment. For 60 patients only the uterus was removed, while for 10 patients one ovary was removed in the operation or had been removed in a prior operation. Women having both ovaries removed were excluded due to possible hormonal after-effects, while a few patients having vaginal hysterectomies or in whom evidence of malignancy was discovered were also excluded. The group was thus more homogeneous than in many other studies, being of one sex and undergoing an identical surgical procedure.

All hysterectomy patients were admitted to one 30-bed ward, under the care of one of three surgeons, with the 70 patients being divided almost equally between them. No patients declined to participate, but two women were excluded because they spoke very little English. Further details of the patients (broken down by intervention condition) are shown in Table 1.

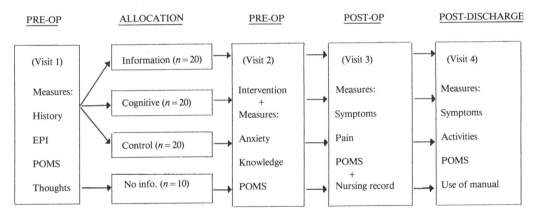

Figure 1. Overview of the design.

Procedure

All patients were seen twice before the operation and twice afterwards, the last interview being three weeks after discharge. The first three visits were in the hospital, while the fourth visit was at the patients' home, except on three occasions when the patient happened to be returning for an out-patient appointment at the time. The first interview was mainly devoted to obtaining background information and base-line measures, although assignment to intervention group was carried out immediately afterwards. All patients requesting information were given a brief manual to read, the contents of which were discussed fully the next day (normally the day before surgery). Visits on the third post-operative day and three weeks post-discharge were used to collect outcome data. All interviews were carried out by one of the authors (VR).

Pre-operative measures (Visit 1). Each patient was contacted on the day of admission and subject to her agreement was interviewed for approximately 40 minutes. In the first part of the interview, personality and mood questionnaires were given (Eysenck Personality Questionnaire, Eysenck & Eysenck, 1964, and Profile of Mood States, Lorr *et al.,* 1967), after which a brief personal history was obtained, including the patient's age, number of previous operations, marital status and degree and frequency of pain experienced leading up to the hysterectomy. Following this a coping questionnaire was administered which inquired about life events over the last 12 months and the type and extent of thoughts concerning the operation. After an initial open question asking for any thoughts relating to surgery, patients were asked to rate how frequently they thought about the operation, and finally to check off any thoughts they recognized from a standard list containing equal numbers of positive and negative thoughts.

Before proceeding further, a check was made on desire for more information about surgery under several headings, sampling preference for procedural information, methods of dealing with anxiety or helping with recovery. Patients were asked to read through a list and to indicate which areas were of interest to them. Unless they failed to indicate a preference for any information ($n = 10$) they proceeded to the next stage, determined by opening a sealed envelope containing the randomly allocated manual.

Intervention conditions. The 20 patients in each of the three intervention conditions were given instruction manuals to read prior to the second pre-operative visit. The manuals were outwardly identical, were of the same length and were introduced with a rationale that reading them would help to set patients at their ease and thus facilitate recovery. The three types of manual differed in the material following this common introduction.

(a) Information: This described the procedures and sensations women were likely to experience before and after the operation, such as skin preparation, pre-medication and the short stay in the recovery room. A diagram showed the spatial relationship of the ovaries, uterus and vagina, and delineated the portion that was to be removed. Immediate post-surgical events were also outlined (e.g. incisional discomfort, possible i.v., catheter, etc.) as well as reassurance being given about the longer-term effects (e.g. return to full activity, sex life, etc.).

(b) Cognitive coping: This suggested that people can control how they view events to some exetent by choosing to dwell on the more positive aspects. Several common worries were presented: 'I am worried about the anaesthetic', followed by statements which minimized the worry: 'Many thousands of people have general anaesthesia every year, they do well and so will I'. The reader was then asked first to supply their own positive thoughts in response to a common worry and secondly, to supply one of their own negative thoughts and then to reappraise the thought in a more positive way.

(c) Attention control: This manual described the ward and the hospital including the routines, staff roles and the location of various amenities. Stress was placed on the fact that the ward was newly opened and had all possible facilities, to maximize both interest and the reassurance provided.

At the back of all three there was a series of questions which were to be answered and then discussed on the second visit. These questions served the dual purpose of assessing how far patients had read and understood the manuals, and also formed a basis for further discussion of material relevant to each particular intervention.

Second pre-operative interview. During the second visit, on the day before the operation, a check was made that the manual had been read, and any questions arising from it were discussed, as well as some additional measures being taken. These measures included a rating of anxiety concerning the operation, and of any worries patients might have had. Additional questions were directed at their knowledge of what was going to happen before, during and after the operation. It was thus possible to estimate the immediate impact made by the different conditions on appropriate target variables, and check that the intervention had the expected psychological effects prior to surgery. Before leaving, the interviewer made sure that the patient had fully understood the contents of the manual, and where appropriate was able to follow any instruction contained in it.

Post-operative measures (Visit 3). During the third visit on the third post-operative day, a series of recovery variables were assessed, including physical symptoms, nausea, vomiting and sleep patterns. Pain levels were measured in three ways: (1) with an analogue scale, (2) with questions about intensity and frequency, and (3) with a scaled checklist of 30 pain descriptors. Mood state was measured by readministration of the mood scale used pre-operatively (POMS).

Finally, all patients were given a diary record form to cover the three-week post-discharge period. They were asked to record five symptoms (nausea, fatigue, pain, irritability and depression) as they occurred, and to note when they first undertook any of 10 household activities derived from a Guttman scale developed by Williams *et al.* (1976).

Post-discharge interview (Visit 4). The fourth and last contact with patients was a home visit conducted three weeks post-discharge. Mood state was once again assessed, and both post-operative symptoms and the resumption of normal activities were determined after a review with each patient of the diary record sheet she had completed. Finally, all intervention patients were asked about their reactions to the manual, and rated its usefulness.

Nursing record measures. Each patient's notes were reviewed and a record made of any comment about post-operative recovery under a number of headings, e.g. pain, temperature, nausea and wound complications. Each specific symptom mentioned was scored one point (e.g. 'patient feels nauseated this morning') and then summed separately under each symptom heading. A complete count was also made of all medications given, classified as antibiotics, analgesics by mouth, or by injection. Sedatives or tranquillizers were counted as analgesics provided they were given to control pain. The number of days stayed in hospital were also recorded.

Results

Analysis

In general, comparisons were made using one-way analyses of variance of between group effects for each pre- and each post-operative measure, both for the three randomly assigned intervention conditions, and all four groups when appropriate (i.e. including the group not requesting information). Covariance analyses, using pre-operative scores as covariates, were employed when measures were taken before and after surgery, for example mood scale scores. Finally a correlational analysis was performed relating all pre-operative to all post-operative measures, both across all groups and within each group separately.

Table 1. Pre-operative means

	Information	Cognitive	Control	No information
Previous operations	2·0	1·9	2·8	1·4
Emotional problems [a]	10/20	8/20	10/20	5/10
EPI 'N' score	12·1	8·8	11·7	11·2
POMS anxiety scores	8·1	8·3	9·8	6·1

[a]Number ever having attended a doctor for an emotional problem.

No significant differences between groups were found on any of the pre-operative measures, including age, marital status, social class, number of children, number of previous operations, neuroticism scores and mood scale scores (see Table 1). The number of positive and negative thoughts reported, and the desire for different kinds of information was also equivalent across all three intervention groups.

Analysis of the data from the second pre-operative visit showed systematic trends for patients' worries or knowledge relating to the type of intervention. Marginally significant differences ($F=3·0$, d.f. $=2,57$, $P=0·06$) were found for ratings of anxiety, with the information and cognitive coping group having lower anxiety scores than the attention control group (see Table 2 for means). Similarly, there was a trend for the cognitive coping group to more frequently deny having worrying thoughts compared with the other randomly allocated groups ($\chi^2 = 5·7$, d.f. $=2$, $P=0·06$).

Although there was a trend for the attention control group to claim less knowledge about the surgical timetable, there was no significant difference overall in answer to a simple yes/no question (see Table 2). When actually asked to list out exactly what would happen during or after surgery, however, striking differences emerged. Each item produced was checked against a standard list of procedures, and one point given for each correct item (an independent reliability check by a judge blind to group membership showed close to 100 per cent agreement). The information group produced the most items, followed by the other intervention groups ($F = 5 \cdot 5$, d.f. $= 2,56$, $P < 0 \cdot 01$). The analysis of all four groups was also significant ($F = 5 \cdot 4$, d.f. $= 3,65$, $P < 0 \cdot 01$), with patients preferring no information knowing least. It is thus clear that the interventions had produced some of the desired effects. The information group knew most about surgery, while both the cognitive coping group and the information group showed a trend towards reduced anxiety levels.

Table 2. Pre-operative intervention effects

	Information	Cognitive	Control	No information
How anxious? (1−4)	1·4	1·45	1·95*	1·67+
Any worries? (% yes)	40%	20%	53%*	30%
Know timetable? (% yes)	85%	75%	53%	90%
Actual items known	4·0	2·6	1·8***	1·3+++

Note. Differences among the randomly allocated groups significant at the $0 \cdot 10$ (*), or $0 \cdot 01$ (***) levels. Differences across all four groups significant at the $0 \cdot 10$ (+), or $0 \cdot 01$ (+ + +) levels.

Post-operative measures. There were no significant differences between groups in self-reported symptoms of nausea, vomiting, pain and amount of sleep during the three days following operation. There was one difference related to sleep disturbance, however, in response to a question about how annoyed patients were about waking up at night ($F = 3 \cdot 5$, d.f. $= 2,57$, $P = 0 \cdot 04$). Both information and cognitive coping groups complained of this less than did the control patients (see Table 3).

Despite the lack of differences in reported pain, evidence of effects on pain was found from the nursing record data. More mention of incisional pain was found in the notes of patients who had refused information ($F = 2 \cdot 8$, d.f. $= 3,66$, $P = 0 \cdot 05$), although differences among the three randomly assigned groups was not significant. Consumption of analgesics showed clear differences, however, in both the three- and four-group analysis. Patients in the cognitive coping group took fewer oral analgesics ($F = 3 \cdot 2$, d.f. $= 2,56$, $P = 0 \cdot 05$), and were given fewer analgesic injections ($F = 3 \cdot 6$, d.f. $= 2,56$, $P = 0 \cdot 04$) than were the other groups, while patients refusing information received most of both types. There were no differences in the number of antibiotics given, or length of stay.

Table 3. Post-operative measures

	Information	Cognitive	Control	No information
Nausea Freq. (0−3)	1·2	1·2	1·7	1·3
Wind Freq. (0−3)	0·9	1·4	1·0	2·0++
Waking Freq. (0−3)	2·0	2·2	2·5	1·8
Annoyed by waking (0−3)	1·6	1·6	2·2**	2·1+
Pain checklist (0−30)	16·9	14·8	18·5	16·9
Pain analogue (0−30)	17·0	15·8	17·4	16·3
Nurses pain observations	3·1	2·5	2·9	5·3++
Temperature (37°C+)	10·9	7·6	7·9	12·2+
Antibiotics	22·7	16·3	17·6	25·1
Oral analgesics	23·8	16·3	24·1**	30·8++
Analgesic injections	4·7	3·8	5·8**	6·1+++

Note. **Differences among the three randomly allocated groups significant at the $0 \cdot 05$ level. Differences across all four groups significant at the $0 \cdot 10$ (+), $0 \cdot 05$ (+ +), or $0 \cdot 01$ (+ + +) levels.

Post-discharge measures. Significant differences between groups were again found on examination of the number of symptoms recorded in the three weeks after discharge. A total score derived from the number of days on which symptoms of each kind were recorded, summed for each patient, showed a marginally significant ($F = 2 \cdot 9$, d.f. = 2,57, $P = 0 \cdot 06$) trend for the cognitive coping group to complain of fewer symptoms than the attention control group, with the information group being intermediate. Separate analyses for each symptom (nausea, fatigue, irritability, depression and pain) revealed significant differences only for days of pain ($F = 3 \cdot 8$, d.f. = 2,57, $P = 0 \cdot 03$), again with cognitive coping patients faring best, and attention control patients worst (see Table 4).

Ten household tasks, approximating a Guttman scale, were recorded on the activity diary sheet for the three-week period, and a score was derived by summing across tasks and number of days each was performed. Analysis of variance showed a non-significant trend across all four groups for the whole three-week period ($F = 2 \cdot 2$, d.f. = 3,66, $P = 0 \cdot 10$), with the cognitive coping group doing most, and the patients who refused information doing least. There were no significant differences among the three randomly allocated groups. Surprisingly in view of the general trend of these results in favour of the cognitive coping condition, patients in the information group rated their manuals as significantly more useful ($F = 7 \cdot 4$, d.f. = 2,55, $P < 0 \cdot 01$) than did patients in the other two relevant conditions (see Table 4).

Table 4. Post-discharge measures

	Information	Cognitive	Control	No information
Total symptoms	29·8	22·3	34·9*	33·6+
Days of pain	9·9	5·9	12·0**	7·5+ +
Total activities	6·6	6·9	5·9	4·6+
Manuals useful? (1 − 5)	4·2	3·1	2·9***	N/A

Note. Differences among the three randomly allocated groups significant at the 0·10 (*), 0·05 (**) or 0·01 (***) levels.
Differences across all four groups significant at the 0·10 (+), or 0·05 (+ +) levels.

Mood scales and correlational analysis. Despite a difference in self-reported concern about the operation, none of the mood scales showed differences across groups, including the tension/anxiety scale. Correlational analyses were equally uninformative, with too few correlations found to be significant for them to be considered beyond chance expectation. There were no convincing indications that pre-operative measures predicted post-operative outcome either across or within groups.

Discussion

The most important finding from this study is that, of the interventions investigated, the cognitive coping strategy was associated with the best outcome. Combined with earlier studies by Langer *et al.* (1975) and Kendall *et al.* (1979) the present results provide fairly powerful evidence that giving standard information about procedures and sensations is a less effective way of promoting recovery from surgery than are other cognitive-behavioural techniques.

Considering first the immediate psychological impact of preparation, the present results demonstrate that while both specific interventions reduced anxiety about the operation, they probably did so in different ways. Patients in the cognitive coping group reported fewer worrying thoughts, while only patients receiving specific information actually knew significantly more about the procedure. Interestingly, patients refusing information also thought they understood the procedure, but actually knew very little about it. This striking mismatch may account for their poor showing on some post-operative variables; for example, high levels of incisional pain and consumption of analgesics. On the other hand, patients who actually received information apparently overestimated how helpful it was, judged by the mismatch between their subjective ratings of usefulness and other indices of recovery.

Not all variables studied revealed any effect due to psychological intervention, and most of those showing effects were self-report measures. This observation raises the question of whether the changes seen are subjective only, with the psychological interventions having little or no effect on physical status or post-operative complications. For example, there were no differences in the number of antibiotic medications given (which may be taken as an index of post-operative complications), and similarly there was no difference in the length of stay in hospital. Nevertheless there was some evidence that patients' communication with staff must have been affected, since differences were found in the number of observational reports of incisional pain by nurses, and in the numbers of analgesics given. Similarly, there was a trend towards behavioural differences in the number of activities performed after discharge, although this did not reach acceptable levels of statistical significance. On present evidence it seems reasonable to conclude that psychological preparation can have both subjective and behavioural effects, which are reflected in different indices of recovery.

The question remains of the mechanism underlying the differential effectiveness of the types of preparation studied. If the effect is thought to be mediated by emotional state, and particularly by anxiety, then it would be necessary to suppose that the cognitive coping method was superior to other methods in reducing anxiety. Although there was some evidence for this from reports of worry about the operation, there was unexpectedly no sign whatsoever of differences in mood state assessed in other ways. It may be that the overall level of anxiety is too blunt a measure of the relevant emotional change, which could consist of a reduction in worries about the operation.

Such a conclusion might help to explain why the cognitive coping method was generally superior to the provision of information about surgery. Although some patients' worries would be countered by the standard information provided, it is inevitable that other patients will have specific individual worries which are not dealt with. The cognitive coping method used here, and by Langer *et al.* (1975), teaches a general strategy which can be applied to any specific worry an individual patient indentifies, and so should help a greater proportion of patients, both before and after surgery. A similar point has been made by Johnston (this issue).

In an earlier review (Mathews & Ridgeway, 1981), we suggested at least three ways in which psychological factors could influence indices of recovery from surgery. Psychological influences might be confined to self-report measures (e.g. via suggestion or demand effects), or could lead to changes in recovery-promoting behaviour (deep-breathing, exercises, mobilization, etc.), or might act directly on physiological or immunological function. If anxiety, for example, has a direct effect on physical function involved in recovery (e.g. via autonomic arousal), then it should not make much difference what the particular focus of that anxiety might be; worry about the operation having similar autonomic effects to worry about anything else. If, on the other hand, the patients' anxiety influences recovery via relevant behavioural consequences (such as showing excessive concern over pain, avoiding activity, etc.) then it is more understandable that the exact form of a patient's worries might be important. Worry about pain, for example, could lead the patient to restrict her activity, and thus retard recovery. Since the interventions used in the present study did not obviously affect overall emotional state, but did reduce worry about the operation, there is no convincing evidence of a direct effect of general emotional state on physical mechanisms of recovery. On the other hand, the evidence that some aspects of patient behaviour were altered (see above) supports the view that successful intervention effects were mediated via behaviour relevant to physical recovery.

Unfortunately, the present data did not appear to help in making advance predictions about which particular patients were in most need of psychological preparation, either standard or tailored to individuals. From our previous review, we had supposed that neuroticism, or trait anxiety, would predict which patients were most vulnerable and therefore in most need of preparation. This supposition did not find support from the present correlational analysis, even when patients from the attention control group alone were examined. Similarly, we had developed a simple measure of cognitive approach-avoidance (a self-rating of frequency of thoughts about the operation) to test the idea that so-called vigilant patients would show a poorer recovery. Earlier pilot work with a group of 20 relatively unprepared hysterectomy patients had shown this measure to be reliable, unrelated to neuroticism, but significantly related to a number of recovery variables. Patients who reported thinking about the operation a great deal had a less good recovery following hysterectomy. This finding was not replicated in the present study regardless of intervention group. Although our pilot results may simply have been unreliable, it is also possible that each of our interventions had sufficient effects to wash out any differences otherwise attributable to personality or cognitive style. Certainly, it would appear that the impact of appropriate psychological intervention is a more powerful influence than that of pre-existing individual differences.

A possible exception to this is provided by the minority of patients who declined information. It is of course impossible to know whether they would have reacted differently to preparation if it was given to them anyway, and all that can be said is that the recovery of such patients in the absence of preparation tended to show a characteristic pattern. As noted above, such patients appear to believe that they knew much more than they did about the surgery, and they also reacted adversely in the immediate post-surgical period; but on the other hand, they did reasonably well after discharge. Possibly these patients could be said to show an avoidant behavioural style, leaving themselves vulnerable to the unexpected (for example the extent of incisional pain) but coping adequately later on when anticipation is less relevant or helpful.

While this leaves little scope for individual selection of those patients in particular need of help, the cognitive coping strategy seems to be flexible enough to be generally applicable to the majority of surgical patients. Since it may be superior in this respect to the type of standard informational preparation which is currently popular, with both clinicians and patients, there are obvious implications for clinical psychologists working in medical or surgical settings. In clinical practice, the relatively modest effects of the present experimentally controlled interventions might well be augmented by combining them. There seems no reason why information, cognitive coping and relaxation techniques could not be combined with other specific behavioural instructions about ways to promote rapid recovery. The development and evaluation of such combinations could usefully be the subject of future research.

Acknowledgements

The authors are very grateful for the help and encouragement given at all stages of this project by Mrs T. Varma, Consultant and Senior Lecturer in the Department of Obstetrics and Gynaecology, at St George's Hospital. We would also like to thank Professor Trussell and Mr Amias of the same department, and the nursing staff of Holdsworth Ward for their generous help.

References

Andrew, J. M. (1970). Recovery from surgery, with and without preparation, for three coping styles. *Journal of Personality and Social Psychology,* **15**, 223–226.

Auerbach, S. M. & Kilmann, P. R. (1977). Crisis intervention: A review of research. *Psychological Bulletin,* **84**, 1189–1217.

De Long, R. D. (1970). Individual differences in patterns of anxiety arousal, stress-relevant information and recovery from surgery. Doctoral dissertation, University of California, Los Angeles.

Egbert, L. D., Battit, G. E., Welch, C. E. & Bartlett, M. K. (1964). Reduction of post-operative pain by encouragement and instruction of patients: A study of doctor–patient rapport. *New England Journal of Medicine,* **270**, 823–827.

Eysenck, H. J. & Eysenck, S. G. B. (1964). *Manual of the Eysenck Personality Inventory.* London: University of London Press.

Hayward, J. (1975). Information — A prescription against pain. *The Study of Nursing Care Projects Reports,* series 2, no. 5. London: The Royal College of Nursing.

Janis, I. L. (1958). *Psychological Stress: Psychoanalytic and Behavioural Studies of Surgical Patients.* New York: Wiley.

Johnson, J. E. (1975). Stress reduction through sensation information. In I. G. Sarason & C. D. Spielberger (eds), *Stress and Anxiety,* vol. 2. Washington: Hemisphere.

Johnston, M. (1980). Anxiety in surgical patients. *Psychological Medicine,* **10**, 145–152.

Kendall, P. C. & Watson, D. (1981). Psychological preparation of stressful medical procedures. In C. Prokop & L. Bradley (eds), *Medical Psychology: Contributions to Medical Psychology.* London: Academic Press.

Kendall, P. C., Williams, L., Pechacek, T. F., Graham, L. E., Shisslak, C. & Herzoff, N. (1979). Cognitive–behavioural and patient education interventions in cardiac catheterization procedures: The Palo Alto medical psychology project. *Journal of Consulting and Clinical Psychology,* **47**, 49–58.

Langer, E. J., Janis, I. L. & Wolfer, J. A. (1975). Reduction of psychological stress in surgical patients. *Journal of Experimental Social Psychology,* **11**, 155–165.

Lorr, M., Datson, P. & Smith, I. R. (1967). An analysis of mood states. *Educational and Psychological Measurement,* **27**, 89–96.

Mathews, A. & Ridgeway, V. (1981). Personality and surgical recovery: A review. *British Journal of Clinical Psychology,* **20**, 243–260.

Melamed, B. G. (1977). Psychological preparation for hospitalisation. In S. Rachman (ed.), *Contributions to Medical Psychology,* vol. 1. Oxford: Pergamon.

Williams, R. G. A., Johnston, M., Willis, L. A. & Bennett, A. E. (1976). Disability: A model and a measurement technique. *British Journal of Preventative and Social Medicine,* **30**, 71–87.

Wilson, J. F. (1981). Behavioral preparation for surgery: Benefit or harm? *Journal of Behavioral Medicine,* **4**, 79–102.

Wilson-Barnett, J. (1979). *Stress in Hospital: Patients Psychological Reactions to Illness and Health Care.* Edinburgh: Churchill Livingstone.

Received 26 April 1982

Requests for reprints should be addressed to Professor Andrew Mathews, Department of Psychology, St. George's Hospital Medical School, Tooting, London SW17 0RE, UK.

Valerie Ridgeway is now at The Cromwell Hospital, Cromwell Road, London SW5.

British Journal of Clinical Psychology (1982), **21**, 281 – 294 *Printed in Great Britain*

Behavioural treatment in the reduction of coronary risk factors: Type A behaviour and blood pressure

D. W. Johnston

The literature on direct behavioural interventions to reduce two coronary risk factors, Type A behaviour and essential hypertension, is reviewed. It is concluded that there is preliminary evidence that the alteration of Type A behaviour is possible and that such alteration is associated with a reduction in the risk of recurrence of myocardial infarction. It is also concluded that reductions in blood pressure can be achieved using behavioural techniques and that such reductions persist for at least 12 months. The exact components of an effective treatment package for essential hypertension are not yet fully established but it is suggested that live relaxation training and stress management techniques are an important part of effective therapy. The positive therapeutic effects obtained in the behavioural treatment of essential hypertension are unlikely to be due to either non-specific effects of therapy or to altered compliance with pharmacological treatment. Reductions in blood pressure of the order obtained in the relaxation and stress management studies could be expected to lead to significant gains in health, including reductions in cardiovascular morbidity, if they are sustained for long periods.

Coronary heart disease (CHD) is a major cause of death in the English speaking world, accounting for almost 40 per cent of deaths in middle-aged men (Levy & Feinleib, 1980). It has been recognized for some time that many of these deaths can be predicted from three classic risk factors: blood pressure, serum cholesterol and cigarette smoking (Levy & Feinleib, 1980), and it is increasingly being argued that a particular pattern of behaviour, Type A behaviour, can be added to this list (Jenkins, 1976). All of these risk factors are either obviously behavioural or are to some extent secondary to behaviours such as inappropriate eating habits. At least two of the risk factors, Type A behaviour and high blood pressure, are of unique psychological interest. The psychological interest of Type A behaviour is clear enough; it is an entirely behaviourally defined risk factor with as yet no known physical basis. The relationship between high blood pressure and behaviour is more subtle but it is increasingly clear that environmental and psychological factors can elevate blood pressure in man and animals through direct neurogenic influence, and it it is widely held that such factors play a role in the aetiology and maintenance of essential hypertension (Steptoe, 1981).

In this paper I shall review the behavioural treatments that have been used to alter Type A behaviour or to lower pressure directly, i.e. independently of other variables such as diet or exercise. There is a certain affinity of aim and technique shared by these topics that makes it appropriate to review them together, and separately from the rather different approach that might be used to control other risk factors by alterations in smoking (Raw, 1977) or diet (Stuart & Davis, 1972). This review will not cover the use of behavioural methods to control the symptoms of coronary heart disease (Johnston, in press).

Type A behaviour

The current interest in the proposition that certain behavioural patterns are intimately linked with coronary heart disease stems largely from the pioneering observations of Friedman & Rosenman (1974) that the pattern they characterized as Type A behaviour is prevalent in patients with ischaemic heart disease. The large and growing literature on the nature, correlates and effects of Type A behaviour (see, for example, Dembroski *et al.,* 1978) testifies to the complexities of the concept, but at its core Type A behaviour is characterized by a chronic struggle to achieve more and more in less and less time. People engaged in this struggle are characterized by a strong achievement orientation, impatience, feelings of being under considerable time pressure, are very emphatic in speech and gesture and often display hostility. People not displaying these characteristics are described as Type B. The originators of the classification developed a brief standardized interview that forms the basis for all other attempts to measure Type A behaviour. The interview and current thinking on Type A behaviour is well summarized by Friedman *et al.* (1981).

Many studies (Jenkins, 1976) have shown that this behaviour pattern is associated with coronary heart disease. However, the most compelling evidence for the association between Type A behaviour and CHD is based on two prospective studies. Rosenman *et al.* (1975) describe the outcome of the Western Collaborative Group Study, in which over 3000 middle-aged men had their behavioural status ascertained by the standardized interview and were then followed up for 8½ years. This study showed that Type A men were approximately twice as likely to develop coronary heart disease as those not displaying the behaviour pattern, and that this was largely independent of the standard risk factors of blood pressure, serum cholesterol and cigarette smoking. Haynes *et al.* (1980) found essentially the same results in a smaller sample of middle-aged men and women characterized as Type A or Type B on a simple questionnaire and studied over an eight-year period. It therefore appears that Type A behaviour does relate to coronary heart disease with a power similar to that of the other risk factors but independently of them. The prevalence of Type A behaviour is unclear; half the sample in the Western Collaborative Group Study were classified as Type A and Friedman *et al.* (1981) have recently claimed that the vast majority of patients surviving a myocardial infarction displayed significant Type A behaviour. If this figure generalizes to other populations then Type A behaviour is a very major risk factor indeed.

Reducing Type A behaviour

Clearly a behavioural risk factor offers a major challenge and opportunity to proponents of behavioural methods of treatment. However, the difficulties in altering Type A behaviour, well described by Roskies (1979), are considerable. The fundamental questions hinge on identifying those aspects of the behaviour which actually carry the risk, and developing effective methods for changing behaviours that both the patient and his culture may value highly. Since the evidence implicating Type A behaviour in coronary heart disease is recent, there are few adequate studies of changing such behaviour. Moreover, with one notable exception, these studies are best regarded as rather tentative preliminary efforts in this direction.

Roskies *et al.* (1978) and Roskies *et al.* (1979) attempted to alter aspects of Type A behaviour in self-selected Type A men. The authors base their treatment on Glass's (1977) analysis of Type A behaviour. This suggests that the pattern results from an overinternalization of a desire to moderate and control one's environment and a resultant feeling of anxiety when such control is lost. Following preliminary screening of 50 volunteers, either a psychoanalytic or a stress management approach was used to treat this anxiety in two groups of healthy Type A men. In addition, a sample of Type A men in whom the screening had revealed evidence of coronary heart disease, were also treated using the stress management techniques. The main outcome measures were blood pressure, serum cholesterol and triglycerides and various measures of anxiety and psychological symptoms. Direct assessment of Type A behaviour was not used as an outcome measure. In an analysis of the subjects without evidence of coronary heart disease, both forms of treatment produced equal change. When the subjects with evidence of coronary heart disease were included in the analysis, it appeared that stress management training produced greater and more stable reduction in some of the measures. However this finding, of course, confounds cardiac state with type of treatment and so may not be all it seems. The authors paid particular attention to the reduction in serum cholesterol, but while this is an interesting and possibly valuable finding in itself, it should be recalled that Type A behaviour is an independent risk factor, and so there is no good reason to believe that the main benefits of changing the behaviour pattern are mediated through a change of cholesterol.

Jenni & Wollersheim (1979) following up some earlier pilot studies of Suinn (1975) and Suinn & Bloom (1978), compared stress management training involving relaxation and the visualization of stressful scenes, with a cognitive therapy based on Ellis's rational emotive therapy (1973). They state that neither of these treatments attempted to change Type A behaviour, but only to reduce the stress which this behaviour occasions. However, this may not be entirely accurate since rational emotive therapy seems an attempt to strike at some of the likely roots of Type A behaviour by, for example, asking subjects to question their particular patterns of goal setting and unrealistic self-statements. The two active treatments and a wait group were compared in a sample of healthy Type A subjects. Self-reported anxiety was reduced in both active treatments but there was no detectable effect on blood pressure or cholesterol. When the sample was subdivided to exclude those subjects with only mild Type A behaviour, it appeared that the cognitive therapy led to reductions in Type A behaviour that did not occur with the stress management or control conditions. However, Type A behaviour was only measured by self-report, so it is therefore quite unsafe to conclude that subjects' behaviour actually changed.

Thoresen *et al.* (1982) have provided preliminary and partial results of a very ambitious study which attempts to modify Type A behaviour and to assess the effects of these modifications comprehensively in a large sample of patients who have experienced at least one myocardial infarction. In a small group setting they attempt to alter behavioural, cognitive, environmental and physiological aspects of the patient's life. The core of their programme is the goal of developing in the patient an awareness of the effects of Type A behaviour in his or her life. The patients then use this awareness to develop and implement techniques for producing appropriate changes in all four aspects of their life. The programme they adopt is complex and draws heavily on most of the techniques current in cognitive behavioural modification. These include self-monitoring, self-reinforcement, modelling, behavioural rehearsal, behavioural contracting and cognitive and environmental restructuring. This comprehensive treatment approach is applied over a five-year period at group meetings which occur at least monthly. The primary comparison in this clinical trial is between the cognitive behavioural treatment plus standard cardiological care or cardiological care alone. The latter was also given in small groups and focuses attention to patients' medication, diet and exercise (but did not include discussion of stress-related behaviour). Over 600 patients have been assigned to 60 cognitive behavioural groups and about 300 similar patients have been assigned randomly to 20 cardiology groups. Thoresen *et al.* have presented preliminary results for the first three years of this five-year project. Already the cumulative reinfarction rate is reliably lower in the group receiving the cognitive behavioural treatment at 7·9 per cent of the sample, compared to 14·6 per cent of those receiving cardiological care only. Type A behaviour, assessed by self-report questionnaire, is measured annually in both treatment conditions, and in addition the patient's spouse and an informant also report on the Type A behaviour of patients receiving the cognitive and behavioural treatment. All three sources of information suggest that Type A behaviour is changing in those receiving psychological treatment, while there is little change in those receiving cardiological care. These findings have been confirmed in a small sample of the patients in both conditions who have also been reinterviewed using the standardized interview for detecting Type A behaviour.

A number of aspects of this study deserve commendation, particularly the large sample of patients in whom the reinfarction rate is likely to be high enough for differences between treatment to be detectable, the use of a comprehensive, but realistic, treatment approach and the care in measuring not just medical outcome but also the putative mediating variable, Type A behaviour. While the results currently available are necessarily far from complete, it is unlikely that the addition of the remaining two years' data will seriously alter them. Of course many questions remain unanswered. It is possible that changes in Type A behaviour may not be the mediating variable since it has been suggested that a variety of different psychological therapies are associated with a reduction in reinfarction rate (Ibrahim *et al.*, 1974; Rahe *et al.*, 1979). Even if it does eventually prove that changing Type A behaviour is possible and relevant, we require much better information on the prevalence of this behaviour before its importance for health in the population at large can be established.

Essential hypertension

As blood pressure rises so does the risk of a number of cariovascular diseases, including coronary heart disease. Kannel (1975) has pointed out that there is no safe level of blood pressure, but for clinical purposes it is convenient to consider blood pressure above a particular level as significant. Most of the studies to be reviewed here take patients whose systolic blood pressure (SBP) is at least 140 mm Hg or whose diastolic (DBP) is 90 or greater. Over 20 per cent of the adult population of the United Kingdom would have blood pressure in this range (Office of Health Economics, 1971), and such levels of pressure are associated with a twofold increase in coronary heart disease and greater increases in other conditions. There are a number of highly effective pharmacological treatments for the reduction of blood pressure and such treatment is associated with a reduction in mortality and morbidity from cardiovascular disease (Veterans Administration Cooperative Study Group, 1967, 1970; Management Committee of the Australian Therapeutic Trial on Mild Hypertension, 1980). However, the strong presumption of the importance of psychological factors in the development and maintenance of hypertension, plus the reluctance of many physicians to place up to 20 per cent of the adult population on lifelong medication and the reluctance of patients to take such medication, has led to the development of a number of psychological treatments for essential hypertension.

Outcome studies

Evaluating the outcome of treatment, especially complex psychological treatment, is always difficult, often controversial and seldom definitive. Successful clinical trials depend on the resolution of the competing requirements of experimental rigour and clinical flexibility, and no single study can hope to do this completely. None of the studies of behavioural treatment for essential hypertension are wholly satisfactory but fortunately they tend to have different deficiencies and so taken collectively enable reasonably strong conclusions to be drawn. In writing this review one primary criterion has been adopted for inclusion of a study, namely that it be based on a random allocation of patients to some form of behavioural treatment and a control condition. Blood pressure is so readily affected by the conditions and frequency of measurement that a simple within-subject design is unlikely to show an interpretable treatment effect.

Table 1 shows the main features of the 13 studies that meet the criterion. It can be seen that all the studies use either cardiovascular biofeedback or, more commonly, some form of relaxation training and stress management or a combination of both.

Relaxation and stress management
The Patel studies. The most impressive series of studies, both in their scale and in their effectiveness, is that described by Patel and her colleagues. The treatment she has developed

consists of a flexible combination of progressive muscular relaxation, meditation, yogic breathing exercises, biofeedback (usually of skin resistance), extensive practice in relaxation at home and in a wide variety of day-to-day situations, and simple training in the self-management of stress. This is supplemented by written material, films and lectures on hypertension and stress. If the uncontrolled or minimally controlled studies of Patel (1975*a*), Patel & Datey (1976) and Patel & Carruthers (1977) are included then this treatment has been used with over 150 hypertensive patients and has been associated with reductions of 21·7 mm in SBP and 13·2 mm in DBP. If primarily due to treatment, then this is an impressive finding of considerable practical significance. Two random allocation studies suggest that this may be the case.

Patel & North (1975) compared the behavioural treatment with regular attendance at the surgery for BP measurement in two groups of hypertensives, most of whom were on medication. There was a marked drop in pressure with therapy which was maintained over a six-month follow-up period. The control group produced a significantly smaller decrease until they too were given the relaxation package, after which they also showed a substantial drop in pressure. In addition to the reduction in pressure, it was possible to reduce some patients' medication. This study included a stress testing condition in which it was shown that the pressor response to dynamic exercise and the cold pressor test was reduced in those who had received the relaxation and stress management package(Patel, 1975*b*).

In a further larger study, Patel *et al.* (1981) described the effects of a group version of this treatment in a sample of unmedicated men, selected from a factory population on the basis of a screening programme. The majority agreed to enter the treatment programme and approximately 200 men were randomly allocated either to the behavioural package or a no-treatment condition. The means for the hypertensive men, approximately 50 per cent of the sample, are shown in Table 1. The treated group clearly show much greater reductions in pressure. The importance of studying patients who are not on medication cannot be overemphasized since it removes the possibility that behavioural treatments act primarily on compliance with medication, which is known to be very poor in some hypertensives.

Controlling for non-specific effects. Patel's studies leave open the possibility that the beneficial effects of the relaxation package stem not from the specific features of the package but from the non-specific care and attention the patients received. This has been examined in three well-conducted studies. Taylor *et al.* (1977) compared progressive muscular relaxation and home practice with supportive psychotherapy or continued medication, in three groups of medicated hypertensives. After five sessions of treatment relaxation was significantly more effective than the alternative treatments and these effects were maintained over a six-month follow-up, although the treatment differences were no longer significant. Brauer *et al.* (1979) compared live progressive muscular relaxation and stress management, very similar to that carried out by Taylor *et al.*, with the same procedure in taped form and also with supportive psychotherapy. Immediately after treatment the three conditions did not differ significantly but at the six-month follow-up the live relaxation condition was significantly better than either taped relaxation or supportive psychotherapy. These results were largely due to the continued improvement in the group receiving live training although they were no longer in contact with their therapists. Very recently the same research group has described the effects of relaxation training on blood pressure measured at frequent intervals throughout the working day, using a semi-automatic ambulatory blood pressure measuring system (Southam *et al.*, 1982). It can be seen from Table 1 that both clinic and ambulatory blood pressure were reduced in the relaxation condition compared to the no-treatment condition. This is a very important finding since it is unlikely that this reflects transient reductions in pressure that could only be produced at the time of measurement in the clinic.

A final major study of the role of non-specific factors in the reduction of blood pressure was described by Bali (1979). In hypertensive volunteers, whose blood pressure was above 130/90 on three separate occasions, Bali compared a combination of progressive muscular relaxation, breathing exercises and verbal feedback of frontalis EMG and breathing patterns with a combination of supportive psychotherapy and psychophysiological measurement. In an attempt to control for the home practice that is common in relaxation training, the subjects in the comparison group were encouraged to rest in bed for 20 minutes per day; unfortunately they quickly gave up this procedure. In this study significant reductions in pressure occurred in the relaxation group that persisted over the 12-month follow-up period. Blood pressure did not alter in the comparison group, but when they went on to have the relaxation package they also showed a substantial reduction in pressure. Bali was particularly concerned to obtain reliable blood pressure measures, so before and after treatment the nine patients in each condition had their blood pressure assessed weekly for eight weeks. On each occasion five BP readings were taken at five-minute intervals. It is unfortunate that the high reliability presumably achieved by this procedure was not necessarily matched by high validity, since the one therapist did all the BP assessments and was therefore, of course, not blind to the patient's treatment. It is also unfortunate that Bali did not use some device such as a random zero sphygmomanometer which might have reduced this potential bias. However, one doubts if therapist bias could be a major effect on 30 blood pressure readings spread over a period of eight weeks.

Meditation

Two studies have compared versions of meditation with control conditions. Seer & Raeburn (1980) carried out a comparison of non-cultic version of transcendental meditation given either with or without a Mantra, and a no-treatment condition in medicated hypertensives. It is quite clear that the addition of a Mantra had no detectable effect and that pressure was reduced more in the meditation than control conditions, although this reached significance only in the case of diastolic pressure. Roberts & Forester (1979) contrasted meditation based primarily on the use of a Mantra with health education classes, with both treatments given in groups. While both approaches were associated with slight reductions in pressure they did not differ reliably. As can be seen in Table 1, the patients in this study did not have particularly high blood pressure and this may well have limited the size of reductions possible.

Cardiovascular biofeedback

The remaining studies all include some form of cardiovascular feedback to aid in the control of blood pressure, either in combination with relaxation training or as the main treatment method. Glasgow *et al.* (1982) describe a study of simple self-relaxation and feedback in both medicated and unmedicated hypertensives. There are two features that distinguish this study; the authors' use of a very simple and apparently practical form of systolic blood pressure feedback and the reliance on extensive blood pressure measurement by the patients themselves as the primary outcome measure. All patients in this study were trained to take their own blood pressure using standard aneroid sphygmomanometers. In addition subjects receiving feedback were trained to use the same apparatus as a simple feedback device. Relaxation training was equally brief and consisted of one session of instruction in the aims and methods of a version of progressive muscular relaxation training which the subjects were then instructed to practise at home. The control group simply monitored their own blood pressure. The complete design for this study consisted of five groups of approximately 15 to 20 hypertensive patients who received either no treatment or four varieties of the behavioural treatment, viz. either four months of relaxation or biofeedback or two months of one treatment followed by two months of the other. The patient's own blood pressure records were supplemented by occasional clinic readings.

Many different BP readings were taken in this study but unfortunately base-line differences between the various conditions made most of the comparisons difficult to interpret. A convincing treatment effect was found only on one measure, the patient's self-recorded BP taken in the afternoon. On this measure there was a significantly greater reduction in SBP and DBP in those patients receiving feedback followed by relaxation when compared with the control group. This effect was true both for the group as a whole and for the subset who were not receiving medication. This interesting combination of feedback and relaxation needs further study, not least because it requires very little professional time, a consideration that is likely to be paramount if behavioural methods are to be accepted as a treatment for such a common condition as mild essential hypertension.

Practically all the studies of conventional laboratory based cardiovascular biofeedback have been disappointing. Elder *et al.* (1973) described a short-term laboratory study comparing two forms of diastolic feedback with a condition in which the patients attempted to lower their pressure without feedback. The subjects were in-patient unmedicated hypertensives. The results of this study are not shown in the table since they were not presented in a comparable form to the other studies tabulated. After eight twice-daily sessions of training the feedback subjects had lower diastolic pressures than the controls (who did not appear to have been at all successful) and the addition of verbal praise to feedback led to significantly greater reductions in pressure. An uncontrolled follow-up study on a very heterogeneous group of out-patient hypertensives did not confirm the power of this technique (Elder & Eustis, 1975). Blanchard *et al.* (1979) used a similar technique to train out-patient hypertensives to control systolic blood pressure. The comparison conditions in this study were frontalis EMG feedback or brief non-specific relaxation instructions. There was no substantial differences between the treatments either in laboratory measures or in blood pressure assessed by a physician. The latter is shown in Table 1.

Table 1. Main outcome measures in randomized controlled trials of behavioural treatments for essential hypertension

Author	n	Treatment	Sessions	Initial BP[a]	BP reduction After treatment	At FU	FU period (months)
(1) Bali (1979)	9	Relaxation, meditation and non-cardiovascular biofeedback	6–10	149/97	12/9	15/11	12
	9	Non-specific support	6–10	150/99	0/1	–	–
(2) Blanchard *et al.* (1979)	10	SBP feedback	12	137/92	2/2	–	–
	9	Frontalis EMG feedback	12	147/101	2/0	–	–
	9	Self relaxation	12	145/87	11/4	–	–
(3) Brauer *et al.* (1979)	10	Live relaxation and stress management	10	153/93	11/6	18/10	6
	9	Taped relaxation and stress management	10	150/95	5/1	–1/5	6
	10	Non-specific support	10	145/93	9/5	2/1	6
(4) Frankel *et al.* (1978)	7	Multiple forms of biofeedback and relaxation training	20	148/99	–3/–1	–	–
	7	False blood pressure biofeedback	20	150/99	1/2	–	–
	8	No treatment	16	151/99	–4/–2	–	–

Author	*n*	Treatment	Sessions	Initial BP[a]	BP reduction After treatment	At FU	FU period (months)
(5) Glasgow *et al.* (1982)[b]	20	No treatment	–	144/95	8/4	–	–
	15–20	Relaxation training	1	141/91	6/5	–	–
	15–20	SBP feedback	1	140/93	8/8	–	–
	15–20	Relaxation training and SBP feedback	2	145/91	10/7	–	–
	15–20	SBP feedback and relaxation training	2	143/93	13/10	–	–
(6) Luborsky *et al.* (1982)	10	Medication	2–5	144/97	16/9	–	–
	16	Relaxation	6	142/93	7/4	–	–
	11	Mild exercise	6	137/95	3/2	–	–
	14	SBP feedback	15	138/90	5/5	–	–
(7) Patel & North (1975)	17	Relaxation, meditation, non-cardiovascular biofeedback and stress management	12	168/100	26/15	21/13	6
	17	Clinic attendance only	12	169/101	9/4	–	–
(8) Patel *et al.* (1981)	50	Relaxation, medication, non-cardiovascular biofeedback and stress management	8	163/100	20/11	22/12	6
	43	No treatment	–	160/100	8/4	11/3	6
(9) Roberts & Forester (1979)	22	Meditation	10	136/84	8/4	–	–
	19	Health education	10	148/87	6/1	–	–
(10) Seer & Raeburn (1980)[c]	14	Transcendental meditation	5	152/104	5/6	2/7	3
	14	Transcendental meditation without mantra	5	147/100	5/7	8/12	3
	13	No treatment	–	150/102	–2/–2	–	–
(11) Southam *et al.* (in press)	21	Relaxation	8	clinic BP 143/98	12/13	–	–
				ambulatory BP 145/95	8/5	–	–
	16	No treatment	–	clinic BP 140/93	4/3	–	–
				ambulatory BP 139/92	0/–2	–	–
(12) Surwit *et al.* (1978)[d]	8	SBP and heart-rate feedback	8	136	–5	–1	1·5
	8	Frontalis EMG feedback	8	134	–11	0	1·5
	8	Relaxation training	8	141	4	5	1·5
(13) Taylor *et al.* (1977)[c]	10	Relaxation	5	150/96	14/5	12/6	6
	10	Non-specific support	5	141/92	3/2	4/4	6
	11	No treatment	5	146/96	1/0	7/2	6

[a] Measures taken on the same occasion have been averaged, e.g. standing, sitting and lying BPs. Reductions are shown as positive numbers.

[b] The measures shown are the patient's records of mid afternoon BP taken from Fig. 6 of Glasgow *et al.*

[c] Substantial loss of patients at follow-up seriously compromises follow-up results.

[d] Only SBP data available from Fig. 2 of Surwit *et al.*

Luborsky *et al.* (1982) also used a form of systolic blood pressure feedback similar to that described by Elder in a study that for the first time compared pharmacological and behavioural treatments. Patients with mild hypertension were assigned to either anti-hypertensive medication (usually a diuretic), systolic blood pressure feedback, a version of progressive muscular relaxation or a control condition. The relaxation technique consisted of taped muscular relaxation training delivered in time to a metronome beating at 60 beats per minute. The control condition was toning up exercises delivered by tape in time with a metronome beating at 130 beats per minute. The exact criteria for inclusion in this study are unclear. It appears that the sample consisted of subjects whose blood pressure either lying or standing was usually above 140/90. Measurement was not blind but was based on readings from a random zero sphygmomanometer. It is clear from Table 1 that medication had the expected effect in this group and that all behavioural treatments were equally ineffective.

Two points may be relevant to this disappointing outcome. Firstly, taped relaxation training was employed (see Brauer *et al.*, 1979); secondly, patients in this study appear to have had somewhat lower blood pressure than the subjects in earlier successful studies of relaxation. This latter point is difficult to document convincingly, because blood pressure was measured under different circumstances in this study from most others.

Only two studies have examined the use of continuous blood pressure feedback. Frankel *et al.* (1978) described a remarkably complex form of treatment that incorporated continuous feedback of diastolic blood pressure and frontalis EMG, autogenic training, progressive muscular relaxation training and between-session home practice in all of these techniques. This was compared to a control condition involving false feedback and a no-treatment condition. None had any systematic effect on blood pressure. Although at first sight it might appear that the treatment offered in this study was comprehensive and potentially powerful, it does seem at least possible that it was too complex and demanding for adequate learning, even in the 20 sessions allotted to it. Patients were measured extensively throughout each training session and after a few preliminary sessions they carried out all four forms of treatment on each session, which lasted up to 1¾ hours. Home practice was almost equally demanding. It does not appear to the present author that this technique is likely either to be conducive to relaxation or appropriate for teaching relaxation, and even the authors of the study admit that it was somewhat inflexible. On the other hand, it must be admitted this was a formally adequate study with comprehensive and careful measurement which failed to show any demonstrable effects of behavioural treatments on blood pressure.

Surwit *et al.* (1978) compared a combination of systolic blood pressure and heart-rate feedback with frontalis EMG feedback and brief relaxation training in mild hypertensives. Again, none of these treatments was associated with any reliable reduction in pressure. It should however be noted that pressure was already low in patients in this study before treatment and we have seen that this may well be a determinant of outcome.

The optimal form of treatment

The effect of blood pressure feedback training in isolation or in combination with relaxation training is therefore disappointing. Only Elder *et al.* (1973) in a brief laboratory study has shown any advantage of feedback over a variety of procedures. These findings may in part reflect the limitations of most of the cardiovascular biofeedback studies reviewed. All the feedback training the patients received in these studies was given when they were at rest in non-arousing environments, and there is an increasing body of evidence that the primary benefits of feedback are seen if training is carried out under arousing conditions (see Johnston *et al.*, 1982; Steptoe, in press). It may also be important that one of the few studies showing a positive effect of cardiovascular feedback was the only one to enable and encourage home practice with the feedback device (Glasgow *et al.*). This technique may both increase the amount of training possible and also enable it to be carried out under more realistic conditions than is possible in the usual psychophysiological laboratory. The rather brief description of therapy provided by most authors plus the lack of relevant comparative studies make it difficult to draw firm conclusions about the essential components of an effective behavioural treatment for hypertension, but the positive studies by Patel, Bali, and the Stanford group (Taylor, Brauer, Agras, etc.) taken collectively suggest that success is most likely to be achieved with live progressive muscular relaxation combined with extensive home practice, the use of relaxation in daily life and active stress management. The latter aspects of treatment should be emphasized; it is unlikely that simply instructing patients in relaxation methods to be practised for limited periods of the day is adequate. Both the research evidence and clinical experience suggest that patients have to be taught how to use these techniques in day-to-day situations and to deal with identifiable stressors in their lives. It is not clear if the addition of any form of non-cardiovascular biofeedback or health education material is helpful but the latter is at least simple and unlikely to be harmful, and could well be incorporated in a comprehensive approach.

Effects on health

There is, as yet, no information on the effects of such behaviourally produced reductions in pressure on cardiovascular mortality. However, if we take the results of Patel's large series of 150 patients as suggesting that SBP can be reduced from 160 to 140 in late middle-aged men, then we can put the reductions in a realistic perspective. Master *et al.* (1952) have shown that the standard deviation of blood presure in men of this age is approximately 18 mm, so this reduction is of the order of one standard deviation. Kannel (1975) has demonstrated that such a reduction would be associated with a drop in the incidence of CHD over an eight-year period from 120 per 1000 to less than 90 per 1000 with, of course, an associated decrease in other cardiovascular diseases. If the hypertensive patients were also high on other risk factors then these reductions would be greater. While the reductions are somewhat smaller in patients with lower initial blood pressure, the number of such patients is much greater and so the consequences for health are considerable. Medication would almost certainly produce larger reductions in pressure but the majority of patients in the above studies were already medicated and so the effects of behavioural treatment and medication appear to be additive. Furthermore, the relationship between blood pressure and risk is not entirely linear and so the larger reductions in pressure are not necessarily associated with equally large reductions in mortality and morbidity. These figures are necessarily only guidelines based on correlational data derived from epidemiological studies. However, the positive outcome of the randomized clinical trials of anti-hypertensive medication encourage the belief that worthwhile gains could be achieved by blood pressure reductions of this magnitude.

Future direction in the treatment of hypertension

While it seems likely that the behavioural method of treatment for high blood pressure will continue to be developed, assessed and practised, a number of critical issues urgently require attention. It is essential that more representative, reliable and valid measures of blood pressure are introduced into the assessment of behavioural treatment. If this is not done, the justifiable suspicion will persist that behavioural treatments simply teach patients the trick of lowering their blood pressure when it is being measured. As a consequence, the relationship between conventional clinic blood pressure and blood pressures throughout the day may differ in the behaviourally treated from the pharmacologically treated. The study by Southam *et al.* referred to earlier is an important step in rectifying this problem. Other methodological problems that require clarification include the dietary stability and drug compliance of patients receiving behavioural treatment. A programme that heightens patients' awareness of the causes and consequences of hypertension (as some of the behavioural treatments explicitly attempt to do) is likely to encourage some patients to alter critical aspects of their life-style or drug compliance, and this may well affect pressure. The effect of diet in particular needs to be more adequately assessed and controlled for than it has been to date (but see Basler *et al.,* 1982).

Assuming that these problems are resolved and behavioural methods of treatment for blood pressure remain attractive, then research should be directed at investigating the critical features of such treatment. This includes the physiological and behavioural mechanisms involved, and the particular patient subgroups that are likely to benefit most from treatment. It is beyond the scope of this paper to review the available research in these topics and, in fact, very little of substance is available. While most assume that relaxation training lowers the sympathetic input to the cardiovascular system (Patel, 1977) direct attempts to test this have had variable results (Stone & DeLeo, 1976; Brauer *et al.,* 1979). Patel *et al.* (1981) have made the very interesting observation that the pattern of change in plasma renin activity found in their study suggested an alteration in the mechanisms involved in the reduction of pressure over the course of training. Attempts to measure possible psychological mechanisms have been inconclusive; for example, Bali (1979) has shown that while relaxation training does lead to reduction of anxiety in hypertensives this reduction is unrelated to a change in pressure. Seer & Raeburn (1980) claim that patients who showed a greater reduction in pressure relaxed more during treatment and felt better able to cope (presumably with stress) after treatment. The samples treated in most studies are too small for prediction of outcome to be a rewarding exercise. The results of Patel *et al.* (1981), Peters *et al.* (1977) and the very useful review paper by Jacobs *et al.* (1977) show quite convincingly that initial blood pressure is a powerful predictor; the higher the pressure the greater the drop. Little else of significance has been reported.

Since it is widely held that essential hypertension is a condition with a multifactorial aetiology that changes with chronicity, it is highly likely that behavioural methods will be most appropriate for only a subset of patients. Steptoe (in press) has argued cogently that treatment should be directed at early labile hypertensives in whom there is a greater cardiac, as opposed to vascular, involvement and in whom neurogenic rather than structural factors are thought to be important. This argument is persuasive and could perhaps be extended to other groups in which sympathetic factors might be critical, such as the hypertensive patients with renin abnormalities (Esler *et al.*, 1977). It cannot be denied however, that behavioural treatment has been very successful in patients with chronic fixed hypertension, and so on both theoretical and empirical grounds there are reasons for believing that a wide variety of hypertensive patients can be appropriately treated by behavioural methods.

As well as seeking a physiological basis for selecting patients, it is also important that patients be selected and properly assessed on behavioural grounds. Behavioural treatments for hypertension at present are applied in ignorance of the actual behavioural, emotional and environmental factors that heighten blood pressure, either in hypertensives in general or in the specific patient. In the best studies some attempts are made to deal with the obvious sources of distress and heightened arousal in the belief that these relate to pressure. This is, however, an untested belief and even if correct may only succeed in enabling the therapist to identify a very limited sample of the situations that actually produce or maintain high pressure. The need for more complete behavioural analysis of the factors associated with high blood pressure is obvious. However, implementing such an analysis with the techniques currently available would be difficult, although probably not impossible. Moreover, improvements in techniques for measuring blood pressure outside the clinic are being sought very actively in many laboratories (Stott *et al.* 1980) and we can expect to see advances in this field that should then be reflected in the assessment and development of behavioural treatments.

Concluding overview

In this paper I have concentrated on two rather restricted topics, the prevention of heart disease by the behavioural treatment of high blood pressure and by altering the Type A behaviour pattern. Much of available evidence is positive and it can be expected that such forms of coronary prevention will be practised increasingly. Furthermore it is possible that behavioural and cognitive approaches will fulfil a major role in preventing coronary heart disease at a much earlier stage, before any aspects of the disease process is manifest, particularly if simple, economic and effective procedures are developed. In addition, it is possible that simple techniques such as relaxation training and stress management might operate on several risk factors simultaneously. There is already suggestive evidence that serum cholesterol as well as blood pressure is reduced by relaxation training (Patel & Carruthers, 1977; Cooper & Aygen, 1979), and it is possible that such training will also have an effect on the major psychosocial risk factors. Given the multiplicative nature of the risk factors for coronary heart disease, the effect on health of these behavioural procedures may be even greater than results of the current studies lead one to hope.

Acknowledgement

This paper was written while the author was supported by the Medical Research Council.

References

Bali, L.R. (1979). Long term effect of relaxation on blood pressure and anxiety levels in essential hypertensive males: A controlled study. *Psychosomatic Medicine,* **41**, 637–646.

Basler, H.-D., Brinkmeier, U., Buser, K., Haehn, K.-D. & Mölders-Kober, R. (1982). Psychological group treatment of essential hypertension in general practice. *British Journal of Clinical Psychology,* **21**, 295–302.

Blanchard, E., Miller, S. T., Abel, C. C., Haynes, M. R. & Wicker, R. (1979). Evaluation of biofeedback in the treatment of essential hypertension. *Journal of Applied Behavior Analysis,* **12**, 99–110.

Brauer, A., Horlick, L. F., Nelson, E., Farquhar, J. U. & Agras, W. S. (1979). Relaxation therapy for essential hypertension: A Veterans Administration outpatient study. *Journal of Behavioural Medicine,* **2**, 21–29.

Cooper, M. J. & Aygen, M. M. (1979). A relaxation technique in the management of hypercholesterolemia. *Journal of Human Stress,* **5**, 24–27.

Dembroski, T. M., Weiss, S. M., Shields, J. L., Haynes, S. G. & Feinleib, M. (1978).*Coronary Prone Behavior.* New York: Springer.

Elder, S. T. & Eustis, N. K. (1975). Instrumental blood pressure conditioning in out-patient hypertensives. *Behavioural Research and Therapy,* **13**, 185–188.

Elder, S. T., Ruiz, R. Z., Deabler, H. J. & Dillenkoffer, R. L. (1973). Instrumental conditioning of diastolic blood pressure in essential hypertensive patients. *Journal of Applied Behavioral Analysis,* **6**, 237–382.

Ellis, A. (1973). *Humanistic Psychotherapy.* New York: Plenum.

Esler, M., Julius, S., Zweifler, A., Randall, O., Harburg, E., Gardiner, H. & Dequattro, V. (1977). Mild high renin essential hypertension. Neurogenic human hypertension. *The New England Journal of Medicine,* **296**, 405–411.

Frankel, B. L., Patel, D. J., Horwitz, D., Friedewald, M. T. & Gaardner, K. P. (1978). Treatment of hypertension with biofeedback and relaxation techniques. *Psychosomatic Medicine,* **40**, 276–293.

Friedman, M. & Rosenman, R. H. (1974). *Type A Behavior and your Heart.* New York: Knopf.

Friedman, M., Thoresen, C. E. & Gill, J. J. (1981). Type A behaviour: Its possible role, detection and alteration in patients with ischaemic heart disease. In J. W. Hurst (ed.), *Update V, The Heart,* pp. 81–100. New York: McGraw Hill.

Glasgow, M. S., Gaardner, K. R. & Engel, B. T. (1982). Behavioural treatment of high blood pressure: II Acute and sustained effects of relaxation and systolic blood pressure biofeedback. *Psychosomatic Medicine,* **44**, 155–170.

Glass, D. C. (1977). *Behaviour Patterns, Stress and Coronary Disease.* Hillsdale, NJ: Erlbaum.

Haynes, S. G., Feinleib, M. & Kannel, W. B. (1980). The relationship of psychosocial factors to coronary heart disease in the Framingham Study: III Eight year incidence of coronary heart disease. *American Journal of Epidemiology,* **111**, 37–58.

Ibrahim, M. A., Feldman, J. G., Sultz, H. A., Staiman, M. C., Young, L. J. & Dean, P. (1974). Management after myocardial infarction: A controlled trial of the effect of group psychotherapy. *International Journal of Psychotherapy in Medicine,* **5**, 253–268.

Jacob, R. G., Kramer, H. G. & Agras, W. S. (1977). Relaxation therapy in the treatment of hypertension. *Archives of General Psychiatry,* **34**, 1417–1427.

Jenkins, C. D. (1976). Recent evidence supporting psychologic and social risk factors for coronary disease. *New England Journal of Medicine,* **294**, 987–994, 1033–1038.

Jenni, M. A. & Wollersheim, J. P. (1979). Cogintive therapy, stress management training and Type A behaviour pattern. *Cognitive Therapy and Research,* **3**, 61–73.

Johnston, D. W. (in press). The behavioural treatment of the symptoms of ischaemic heart disease. In R. Surwit, R. Williams & A. Steptoe (eds.), *The Behavioral Treatment of Disease.* New York: Plenum.

Johnston, D. W., Lo, C. R., Marie, G. V. & Van Jones, J. (1982). Self control of interbeat interval and pulse transit time at rest and during exercise. A preliminary report. *Acta Medica Scandinavica, Supplement,* **660**, 238–243.

Kannel, V. B. (1975). Role of blood pressure in cardiovascular diseases: The Framingham study. *Angiology,* **26**, 1–14.

Levy, R. I. & Feinleib, M. (1980). Risk factors for coronary heart disease and their management. In E. Braunwald (ed.), *Heart Disease: A Textbook of Cardiovascular Medicine,* pp. 1247–1278. Philadelphia: Saunders.

Luborsky, L., Crits–Cristeph, P., Brady, J. P., Kron, R. E., Weiss, T., Cohen, M. & Levy, L. (1982). Behavioural vs. pharmacological treatment for essential hypertension: A needed comparison. *Psychosomatic Medicine* **44**, 203–213.

Management Committee of the Australian Therapeutic Trial in Mild Hypertension. (1980). *Lancet,* **1**, 1261–1267.

Master, A. M., Garfield, C. I. & Walters, M. B. (1952). *Normal Blood Pressure and Hypertension.* London: Henry Kimpton.

Office of Health Economics. (1971). *Hypertension: A Suitable Case for Treatment.* London: Office of Health Economics.

Patel, C. (1975a). 12 month follow-up of yoga and feedback in the management of hypertension. *Lancet,* **i**, 62–64.

Patel, C. (1975b). Yoga and biofeedback in the management of 'stress' in hypertensive patients. *Clinical Science and Molecular Medicine,* **48**, *Supplement,* 171–174.

Patel, C. (1977). Biofeedback-aided relaxation and meditation in the management of hypertension. *Biofeedback and Self-Regulation,* **2**, 1–41.

Patel, C. & Carruthers, M. (1977). Coronary risk factor reduction through biofeedback-aided relaxation and meditation. *Journal of the Royal College of General Practitioners,* **27**, 401–405.

Patel, C. & Datey, K. K. (1976). Relaxation and biofeedback techniques in the management of hypertension. *Angiology,* **27**, 106–113.

Patel, C. & North, W. R. S. (1975). Randomised controlled trial of yoga and biofeedback in the management of hypertension. *Lancet,* **ii**, 93–95.

Patel, C., Marmot, M. G. & Terry, D. J. (1981). Controlled trial of biofeedback-aided behavioural methods in reducing mild hypertension. *British Medical Journal,* **282**, 2005–2008.

Peters, R. K., Benson, H. & Peters, J. M. (1977). Daily relaxation breaks in a working population: 11 Effects on blood pressure. *American Journal of Public Health,* **67**, 954–959.

Rahe, R. H., Ward, H. W. & Hayes, V. (1979). Brief group therapy in myocardial infarction rehabilitation: Three to four year follow-up of a controlled trial. *Psychosomatic Medicine,* **41**, 229–242.

Raw, M. (1977). The psychological modification of smoking. In S. Rachman (ed.), *Contributions of Medical Psychology,* vol. 1, pp. 189–210. London: Pergamon.

Roberts, B. & Forester, W. E. (1979). Group relaxation: Acute and chronic effects on essential hypertension. *Cardiovascular Medicine,* 375–380.

Rosenman, R. H., Brand, R. J., Jenkins, C. D., Friedman, M., Straus, R. & Wurm, M. (1975). Coronary heart disease in the Western collaborative group study. Final follow-up experience of 8½ years. *Journal of the American Medical Association,* **233**, 872–877.

Roskies, E. (1979). Considerations in developing a treatment programme for the coronary-prone (Type A) behavior pattern. In P. Davidson (ed.), *Behavioral Medicine: Changing Health Life Styles,* pp. 295–333. New York: Brunner/Mazel.

Roskies, E., Spevack, M., Surkis, A., Cohen, C. & Gilman, S. (1978). Changing the coronary-prone (Type A) behaviour pattern in a non-clinical population. *Journal of Behavioral Medicine,* **1**, 201–216.

Roskies, E., Kearney, H., Spevack, M., Surkis, A., Cohan, C. & Gilman, S. (1979). Generalizability and durability of treatment effects in an intervention programme for coronary-prone (Type A) managers. *Journal of Behavioral Medicine,* **2**, 195–207.

Seer, P. & Raeburn, J. M. (1980). Meditation training and essential hypertension: A methodological study. *Journal of Behavioral Medicine,* **3**, 59–73.

Southam, M. A., Agras, W. S., Taylor, C. B. & Kraemer, H. C. (1982). Relaxation training: Blood pressure lowering during the working day. *Archives of General Psychiatry,* **39**, 715–717.

Steptoe, A. (1981). *Psychological Factors in Cardiovascular Disorder.* London: Academic Press.

Steptoe, A. (in press). Control of cardiovascular reactivity in the treatment of hypertension. In R. Surwit, R. Williams & A. Steptoe (eds), *The Behavioral Treatment of Disease*. New York: Plenum.

Stone, R. A. & DeLeo, J. (1976). Psychotherapeutic control of hypertension. *New England Journal of Medicine*, **294**, 80–84.

Stott, F. D., Raftery, R. B. & Goulding, L. (1980). *Isam 1979*. London: Academic Press.

Stuart, R. B. & Davis, B. (1972). Slim chance in a fat world: Behavioural control of obesity. Champaign, IL: Research Press.

Suinn, R. M. (1975). The cardiac stress management programme for Type A patients. *Cardiac Rehabilitation*, **5**, 13–15.

Suinn, R. M. & Bloom, L. J. (1978). Anxiety management training for pattern A behaviour. *Journal of Behavioral Medicine*, **1**, 25–35.

Surwit, T. S., Shapiro, D. & Good, M. I. (1978). Comparison of cardiovascular biofeedback, neuromuscular biofeedback and meditation in the treatment of borderline essential hypertension. *Journal of Consulting and Clinical Psychology*, **46**, 252–263.

Taylor, C. B., Farquhar, J. W., Nelson, E. & Agras, W. S. (1977). Relaxation therapy and high blood pressure. *Archives of General Psychiatry*, **34**, 339–342.

Thoresen, C. E., Friedman, M., Gill, J. K. & Ulmer, D. K. (1982). The recurrent coronary prevention programme: Some preliminary findings. *Acta Medica Scandinavica, Supplement*, **660**, 172–192.

Veterans Administration Co-operative Study on Antihypertensive Agents (1976). Effects of treatment on morbidity in hypertension: I. Results in patients with diastolic blood pressure averaging 115 through 129 mm Hg. *Journal of the American Medical Association*, **202**, 1028–1034.

Veterans Administration Co-operative Study on Antihypertensive Agents (1970). Effects of treatment on morbidity in hypertension: II. Results in patients with diastolic blood pressure averaging 90 through 114 mm Hg. *Journal of the American Medical Association*, **213**, 1142–1152.

Received 17 March 1982

Requests for reprints should be addressed to Dr D. W. Johnston, Psychological Treatment Research Unit, The Warneford Hospital, Oxford, OX3 7JX, UK.

British Journal of Clinical Psychology (1982), **21**, 295 – 302 *Printed in Great Britain*

Psychological group treatment of essential hypertension in general practice

Heinz-Dieter Basler, Ulrich Brinkmeier, Kurt Buser, Klaus-Dieter Haehn
and **Regine Mölders-Kober**

One hundred and seven obese patients with essential hypertension from eight general practices received one of the following psychological group therapy procedures: (1) modification of nutritional patterns; (2) modification of nutritional patterns plus self-monitoring of blood pressure and training in social competence; (3) modification of nutritional patterns plus Jacobson's relaxation training; (4) information about the causes and consequences of high blood pressure. An approximately equal number of patients served as a waiting-control group. All patients had received pharmacological treatment for at least a year. Each procedure was administered by a psychologist with groups of up to 15 patients in 12 weekly sessions. The blood pressure values measured before and after intervention showed a clear reduction; this fall is greatest when the initial values were high. Even when the magnitude of the initial values was statistically controlled there was a distinctly greater reduction in blood pressure in the treatment groups than in the waiting-control group. No differential effect between the various therapy procedures could be demonstrated, however. The changes in general health behaviour of the treatment groups was statistically confirmed. In addition, there was a distinct reduction in body weight. Medication compliance also improved in the treatment groups. Since group procedures were accepted both by the doctors and the patients involved, they should be included to a great extent in the basic care of hypertensive patients in the future.

Since behavioural-therapeutic methods have proved effective in the treatment of essential hypertension in clinically controlled studies, it seems appropriate to check whether these methods are also effective in lowering blood pressure under the conditions of general practice (Sackett *et al.*, 1975; Benson *et al.*, 1977; Shapiro & Goldstein, 1980; Wechsler *et al.*, 1980).

Only when psychological therapy methods can be successfully integrated into basic medical care will they be useful in the treatment of this widespread disease. Several procedures have so far proved effective in the treatment of high blood pressures, including modification of nutritional patterns (Basler & Schwoon, 1977; Pudel, 1978; Wechsler *et al.*, 1980), self-monitoring of blood pressure combined with training to overcome stress (Benson *et al.*, 1971; Carnahan & Nugent, 1975; Blanchard *et al.*, 1979; Shapiro & Goldstein, 1980), and relaxation procedures (Blackwell *et al.*, 1976; Benson *et al.*, 1977; Beiman *et al.*, 1978; Brauer *et al.*, 1979; Agras *et al.*, 1980). The effectiveness of supplying information about hypertension and cardiac risks has not yet been unequivocally clarified (Sackett *et al.*, 1975; Levine *et al.*, 1979; Basler, 1980).

In the study described here, we investigated the following questions:

(1) In addition to the reductions brought about by medication, can the blood pressure of obese persons with essential hypertension be further reduced by psychological group procedures in the general practice setting?

(2) What effect do psychological group procedures have on body weight, health behaviour and compliance?

(3) Can differential effects be seen between the various methods employed?

Method

A total of 209 obese essential hypertensives (at least 10 per cent overweight) who had been treated for at least one year with various antihypertensive agents in eight general practices in Hannover were included in the study. The patients in each practice were divided into a therapy group and a waiting-control group, so that a total of eight therapy groups was formed. The prospect of psychological supervision was held out for the waiting groups. Pairs of therapy groups were treated with the same procedure, hence making it possible to investigate four different forms of therapy.

0144-6657/82/040295 – 08 $02.00/0 © 1982 The British Psychological Society

Treatments

(1) A behavioural-therapeutic obesity training programme primarily aiming at the change of eating habits ($n = 25$). The following aspects were dealt with during group meetings: (*a*) encouragement of mutual assistance, (*b*) entering a therapeutic contract, (*c*) involvement and support by a therapeutic counsellor, (*d*) information on health problems, (*e*) survey of undesirable eating behaviour, (*f*) change of eating habits in small steps according to predetermined rules, (*g*) self-assessment of success and its documentation, (*h*) strengthening of desirable eating habits according to the principles of operant conditioning, (*i*) a systematic build-up of alternative behaviour by role playing, (*j*) a programme aimed at increasing activity.

(2) In addition to a shortened version of the obesity training programme, this treatment included self-monitoring of blood pressure to diagnose pressor situations as well as stress management training by means of role play ($n = 27$). The following therapeutic steps were included:
(a) learning to measure one's own blood pressure, (*b*) regular self-monitoring with the aim of producing a daily diagnosis, (*c*) analysis of these results and the accompanying situations with an aid of a diary sheet, (*d*) working out individual connections between situations and blood pressure levels, (*e*) identification of situations leading to higher blood pressure and engagement in role play in order to develop alternative behaviour with which to master such situations, (*f*) practice of role play in the group and modification of the behaviour through group feedback, (*g*) translation of these newly acquired behaviours into real life situations.

(3) In addition to an abbreviated obesity training, this group was given relaxation training according to Jacobson ($n = 27$). The training goal consisted of learning relaxation and applying this skill in situations that provoke pressure reactions. The following elements were included: (*a*) training in relaxation, (*b*) information on stress theory, (*c*) recognition of stress-inducing situations, apparently leading to increases in blood pressure, (*d*) discussion of stress situations in the group, (*e*) application of relaxation in real situations.

(4) Provision of information with the goal of motivating changes of behaviour ($n = 28$). The following items of information were included: (*a*) anatomy and function of the heart-circulatory system, (*b*) effects and side-effects of medication, (*c*) food, especially consumption of salt, (*d*) bodily activity, (*e*) smoking and alcohol, (*f*) stress, (*g*) relaxation, rest, vacation.

All these procedures were carried out by clinical psychologists with a maximum of 15 patients in the doctors' waiting rooms. For each group there were 12 sessions lasting 1½ hours at weekly intervals. Before the intervention, which took place in the second quarter of 1980, and again five to six months after the conclusion of the intervention, the patients were questioned on their health behaviour and compliance by means of a standardized interview. In addition, socio-demographic data were collected. Blood pressure was measured during and upon conclusion of the interview. In addition, blood pressures measured and documented by the attending physicians during the period January 1979 to December 1980 were analysed.

Results

Description of the sample

The mean age of the patients was 51 years (SD $\pm$ 10·5). There was a preponderance of women (60 per cent), and 80 per cent of all patients were married. One quarter had attended a school leading to further education (technical school, grammar school); 57 per cent were classified as lying within lower social groups and 43 per cent in middle class groups (Kleining & Moore, 1968). The differences between the test groups and the waiting-control groups with regard to these characteristics were not statistically significant.

Blood pressure changes

Figures 1 and 2 show the pattern of the mean blood pressures per quarter year measured by the attending physicians. It can be seen that although the blood pressure is apparently subject to seasonal variations, after intervention the blood pressure of the treatment groups is clearly below that of the waiting-control group. This gives grounds for thinking that an effect was produced by the interventions. It is evident that blood pressure fell not only in the treatment groups, but also in the waiting-control group, although the modification in the latter cannot be statistically confirmed.

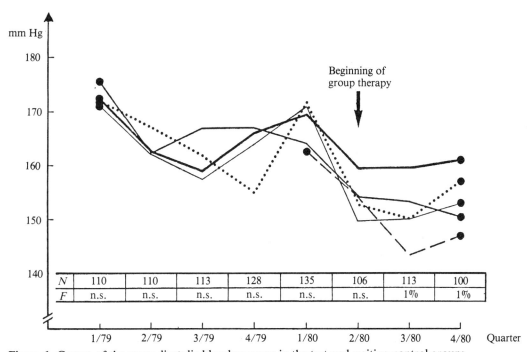

N	110	110	113	128	135	106	113	100
F	n.s.	n.s.	n.s.	n.s.	n.s.	n.s.	1%	1%

Figure 1. Course of the mean diastolic blood pressure in the test and waiting-control groups (significance test by simple variance analysis). ●━━●, control group; ●– – –●, obesity; ●·······●, obesity + self-management; ●━━●, obesity + relaxation; ●━━●, information.

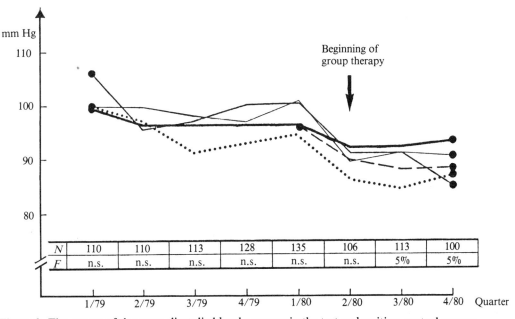

N	110	110	113	128	135	106	113	100
F	n.s.	n.s.	n.s.	n.s.	n.s.	n.s.	5%	5%

Figure 2. The course of the mean diastolic blood pressure in the test and waiting-control groups (significance test by simple variance analysis). ●━━●, control group; ●– – –●, obesity; ●·······●, obesity + self-management; ●━━●, obesity + relaxation; ●━━●, information.

Since there was a significant correlation at the 1 per cent level between the magnitude of the blood pressure difference and the initial blood pressure value in the first quarter of 1980 (r syst. $= 0 \cdot 54$; r diast. $= 0 \cdot 49$), we carried out covariance analysis in which the form of therapy was inserted as a factor and the initial values as covariates.

Table 1. The influence of the covariable 'initial blood pressure' on the difference between the mean systolic blood pressures in the first and fourth quarters of 1980

	Initial systolic values			Deviation from the grand mean of the difference	Corrected deviation covariable: initial values
	M	S	N		
1. Obesity	160·1	18·2	15	−1·77	−6·26
2. Obesity + self-measurement	172·9	15·2	16	−4·09	−1·10
3. Obesity + relaxation	172·1	10·5	15	−7·90	−5·39
4. Information	163·9	15·6	8	−1·27	−3·54
5. Control	167·8	15·3	35	+6·30	+6·31

$F = 3·732$; d.f. = 4,84; $P<0·01$.
Grand mean = −11·10;   explained variance: $R^2 = 0·40$.

Table 2. The influence of the covariable 'initial blood pressure' on the difference between the mean diastolic blood pressures in the first and fourth quarters of 1980

	Initial diastolic values			Deviation from the grand mean of the difference	Corrected deviation covariable: initial values
	M	S	N		
1. Obesity	95·5	10·7	15	−1·83	−2·37
2. Obesity + self-measurement	94·7	8·3	16	−0·93	−1·92
3. Obesity + relaxation	102·1	9·5	15	−5·03	−1·80
4. Information	99·1	7·4	8	−7·99	−6·47
5. Control	94·6	7·1	35	+5·19	+4·14

$F = 3·094$; d.f. = 4,84; $P<0·05$.
Grand mean = −5·51;   explained variance: $R^2 = 0·34$.

Table 3. Change of blood pressure between the first and fourth quarter 1980 — physician's measurements — in the therapy groups in comparison with the control group in regard to the initial blood pressure value (covariance analysis)

		d.f.	F	P
1. Obesity	syst.	1·47	10·435	0·01
	diast.	1·47	5·410	0·05
2. Obesity + self-measurement	syst.	1·48	2·976	0·1>P>0·09
	diast.	1·48	5·352	0·05
3. Obesity + relaxation	syst.	1·47	8·549	0·01
	diast.	1·47	3·973	0·05
4. Information	syst.	1·40	4·743	0·05
	diast.	1·40	9·306	0·01
5. All therapy groups together	syst.	1·86	13·808	0·01
	diast.	1·86	11·008	0·01

From Tables 1 and 2 we see the blood pressure differences between the first and fourth quarter in the individual groups when the initial values are statistically controlled. The mean blood pressure difference for all groups (grand mean) was −11·10 systolic and −5·51 diastolic. The mean values in the test groups were even more greatly reduced while the changes in the control groups were less. Even after correction for initial levels, therefore, the differences between the treatment and control groups were significant. A further covariance analysis is shown in Table 3, in which reductions in blood pressure found in therapy groups are compared with those of the control group. Here again the blood pressure reductions in all therapy groups were significantly different from those in the control group. Comparisons of each single therapy group with the waiting-control group generally showed statistically significant differences. In the obesity + self-monitoring condition there were no differences in systolic values; however, as far as the diastolic reading is concerned the differences with the waiting-control group were reliable.

Changes in medication

Although the doctors were requested not to change the medication of their patients during the course of the study, only 57·9 per cent of the patients stated that medication was unchanged at the second interview. There had been a change to another drug in 22·9 per cent, an increase in the dosage of the same drug in 2·4 per cent and a dosage reduction or complete withdrawal in 16·8 per cent. However, the type of change was distributed equally between the treatment and control groups ($\chi^2 = 1·02$; d.f. $= 1, 0·50 > P > 0·30$). There was a statistically unconfirmed tendency for medication in the information group to remain unchanged more frequently than in the other groups. On the whole, no differential influence of changes in medication on the various groups could be demonstrated, so in the present analysis, the influence of changes in medication on reductions in blood pressure need not be taken into account.

The alteration in weight, health behaviour and compliance

Since there was a significant correlation between the original weight and the weight difference ($r = 0·39$, $P < 0·01$), a covariance analysis on the weight differences, standardized by bodily height was carried out in different groups (Table 4). Differential weight changes persisted despite this correction. A further convariance analysis (Table 5) shows that the weight reduction of all therapeutic groups considered together was significantly greater than that of waiting-control group ($F = 9·537$, d.f. $= 1,154$, $P < 0·01$). When examining the reduction of weights in the individual therapeutic groups it is evident that all showed greater changes than controls with the exception of the information group. An influence of the interventions on general health behaviour (smoking and drinking habits, physical activity, participation in screening examinations) was confirmed when all the treatment groups were compared with the control group (covariance analysis: $F = 4·247$, d.f. $= 1,131$, $P < 0·05$). The greatest change in general health behaviour within the treatment groups was found in

Table 4. Influence of the covariable 'initial weight' (Broca-Index) on the difference between the mean Broca-Index values at the first and second interview

	Initial body weight			Deviation from the grand mean of the difference	Corrected deviation covariable: initial values
	M	S	N		
1. Obesity	170·4	39·8	21	−6·28	−3·63
2. Obesity + self-measurement	145·4	17·2	26	−3·56	−3·87
3. Obesity + relaxation	144·7	25·1	24	−1·02	−1·42
4. Information	142·0	16·7	26	+2·08	+1·37
5. Control	145·3	27·9	60	+3·24	+2·92

$F = 3·712$; d.f. $= 4,152$; $P < 0·01$.
Grand mean $= -3·62$; explained variance: $R^2 = 0·21$.

Table 5. Change of weight (Broca-Index) in the therapy groups between the first and second interview compared to the waiting-control group with regard to the initial weight (covariance analysis)

	F	d.f.	P
1. Obesity	5·676	1·78	<0·05
2. Obesity + self-measurement	10·812	1·83	<0·01
3. Obesity + relaxation	3·966	1·81	=0·05
4. Information	0·411	1·83	0·6>P>0·5
5. All therapy groups together	9·537	1·154	<0·01

the information group (t test for paired differences: $t = 2·09$, d.f. $= 19$, $P = <0·05$). The changes in the other treatment groups were not significant.

We ascertained medication compliance indirectly by suggesting reasons at the second interview for possibly taking medicaments irregularly (fear of habituation, after drinking alcohol, when one feels better, etc.). The patients were asked to say whether they had omitted their medication recently for these reasons. Patients who claimed not to have omitted medications for any of the reasons given above were termed compliant. According to these strict criteria, only 54 per cent of the patients were compliant. There were, however, statistically significant differences between the treatment groups (61 per cent compliance) and the control group (43 per cent compliance: $\chi^2 = 5·42$, d.f. $= 1$, $P<0·05$). Hence, a positive influence of group therapy on compliance can be inferred.

Among the individual experimental groups, however, no differences in compliance rates were found.

Therapy drop-outs

Of the 107 patients who commenced group therapy, 29 (27 per cent) attended six or fewer sessions. We termed these patients therapy drop-outs. If we compare these patients with those who attended all the sessions we find clear differences with regard to weight reduction. In the drop-outs the weight difference was only $-0·3$kg whereas in those successfully completing the course ($n = 30$) it was $-7·1$kg ($t = 4·3$; d.f. $= 56$, $P< 0·01$). Variations in blood pressure differences between the two groups were more noticeable for the values measured at the interview than for those measured by the doctor.

The differential effect of the methods

Although the treatment groups clearly differ from the waiting-control group in blood pressure and weight reductions, the differences between the individual therapeutic procedures were slight. A covariance analysis (with initial values as the covariate) in which only the four therapy groups were included yielded no significant differences among groups for weight reduction, systolic or diastolic blood pressure. Hence a differential effect between the various experimental conditions on weight or blood pressure could not be demonstrated with any certainty.

Discussion

Psychological group programmes, utilized in a general practice setting, produce distinct reductions of blood pressure over and above those seen with medical therapy. Our failure to confirm statistically the effects of obesity training + self-monitoring on systolic pressure reductions may be due to the fact that immediately after completion of therapy, the blood pressure measuring apparatus was withdrawn. This possibility is supported by the observation that during the therapy, the blood pressure reduction in this group was the highest, and the subsequent relapse greatest (Figs 1 and 2).

Blood pressure reductions may be accompanied by decreases in body weight and only in the information group did the body weight fail to decrease significantly. We explain this by the fact that only in this condition were group behaviour modification techniques not applied to weight reduction. Information alone about the risks of being overweight and on the possibilities of weight reduction do not effect appropriate change of behaviour. The information group was however able to reduce blood presure, which may have been due to changes in other blood pressure relevant risk factors (for instance the general health behaviour).

The greatest reductions in both weight and blood pressure were found in persons with high initial values. Change in the general health behaviour due to group work could also be statistically confirmed, and this was seen most clearly in the information group.

The reduction in blood pressure cannot be linked with changes in medication. Although contrary to the original plan of the study the medication was frequently changed, these changes were distributed to the same extent among all groups. However, a relationship with improved medication compliance can be seen. The treatment groups showed better compliance than the control group. Without doubt this, together with improved health behaviour, explains part of the observed reduction in blood pressure. Compliance concerning participation in the group sessions also influenced therapeutic success. Drop-outs had a poorer response than persons who regularly attended the sessions.

A differential effect of the individual group procedures could not be confirmed. Hence, it appears that the attention received and motivation to cooperate in the therapy brought about by group work were the main factors in producing the therapeutic gains. Since psychological group procedures can be carried out in the general practice setting and are accepted by both the patients and the doctors involved, it appears justified on the basis of the results of this study to call for increased integration of such procedures into the basic care of essential hypertensives in the future.

Acknowledgements

This research was supported by Boehringer Mannheim and the Federal Minister for Research and Technology.

References

Agras, S.W., Taylor, C.B., Kraemer, H.C., Allen, R.A. & Schneider, J.A. (1980). Relaxation training: Twenty-four-hour blood pressure reductions. *Archives of General Psychiatry*, 37, 859.

Basler, H.-D. (1980). Klinisch psychologische Interventionsmöglichkeiten im präventiven Bereich. In T. Schneller *et al.*, *Medizinische Psychologie* III, pp. 38–60. Stuttgart: Kohlhammer.

Basler, H.D. & Schwoon, D.R. (1977). Verhaltenstherapie und zugrundeliegende Lerntheorie. In H.E. Bock, W. Gerok & F. Hartmann (eds), *Klinik der Gegenwart*, 11, pp. 664–676. München: Urban & Schwarzenberg.

Beiman, I., Graham, L.E. & Ciminero, A.R. (1978). Setting generality of blood pressure reductions and the psychological treatment of reactive hypertension. *Journal of Behavioral Medicine*, 1, 445.

Benson, H., Kotch, J.B., & Crassweller, K.D. (1977). The relaxation response: A bridge between psychiatry and medicine. *Medical Clinics North America*, 61, 929.

Benson, H., Shapiro, D., Tursky, B. & Schwartz, G.E. (1971). Decreased systolic blood pressure through operant conditioning techniques in patients with essential hypertension. *Science*, 173, 740.

Blackwell, B., Bloomfield, S., Gartside, P., Robinson, A., Hanneson, I., Magenheim, H., Nidick, S. & Zigler, R. (1976). Transcendental meditation in hypertension: Individual patterns. *Lancet*, i, 223.

Blanchard, E.B., Miller, S.T., Abel, G.G., Haynes, M.R. & Wicker, R. (1979). Evaluation of biofeedback in the treatment of borderline hypertension. *Journal of Applied Behavioral Analysis*, 12, 99.

Brauer, A.P., Horlik, L., Nelson, E., Farquhar, J.W. & Agras, W.S. (1979). Relaxation therapy for essential hypertension: A veterans administration outpatient study. *Journal of Behavioral Medicine*, 2, 21.

Carnahan, J.E. & Nugent, C.A. (1975). The effects of self-monitoring by patients on the control of hypertension. *American Journal of Medical Science*, 269, 69.

Kleining, G. & Moore, H. (1968). Soziale Selbsteinstufung (SSE). *Kölner Zeitschrift für Soziologie und Sozial-psychologie*, 20, 502.

Levine, D.M., Green, L.W., Deeds, S.G., Chwalow, J., Russell, R.P. & Finlay, J. (1979). Health education for hypertensive patients. *Journal of the American Medical Association,* **241,** 1700.

Pudel, V. (1978). *Zur Psychogenese und Therapie der Adipositas.* Berlin: Springer.

Sackett, D.L., Gibson, E.S., Taylor, D.W., Haynes, R.B., Hackett, B.C., Roberts, R.S. & Johnson, A.L. (1975). Randomised clinical trial of strategies for improving medication compliance in primary hypertension. *Lancet,* **i,** 1205.

Shapiro, D. & Goldstein, I.B. (1980). Verhaltensmuster und ihre Beziehung zur Hypertonie. In J. Rosenthal (ed.), *Arterielle Hypertonie,* pp. 12–25. Berlin: Springer.

Wechsler, J.G., Schönborn, J. & Ditschuneit, H. (1980) Übergewicht und Blutdruck. In J. Rosenthal (ed.), *Arterielle Hypertonie,* pp. 26–40. Berlin: Springer.

Received 2 January 1982; revised version received 14 May 1982

Requests for reprints should be addressed to Professor Heinz-Dieter Basler, Zentrum für Öffentliche Gesundheitspflege, Medizinische Hochschule Hannover, Karl-Wiechert-Allee 9, 3000 Hannover, 61, West Germany.

British Journal of Clinical Psychology (1982), **21**, 303 – 311   *Printed in Great Britain*

Essential hypertension and psychological functioning: A study of factory workers

Andrew Steptoe, Donald Melville and **Alvin Ross**

This study was designed to examine the links between psychological characteristics and mild essential hypertension. Hypertensives were identified through mass screening of industrial populations. Sixteen men under the age of 56 whose blood pressure remained above 145/90 (145/95 for the 45 – 55 age group) on three separate occasions were compared with 13 age-matched normotensives from the same population. Participants completed a series of personality questionnaires, and carried out concurrent mood ratings and blood pressure self-monitoring four times daily for 14 days. Subjects remained unaware of their diagnostic status until the procedure was completed. No differences between groups were found on measures of trait anxiety, total hostility or direction of hostility. State anxiety and Type A (coronary-prone) scores were significantly higher in normotensives than in hypertensives. Analysis of mood and self-monitored blood pressure revealed consistent correlations between negative mood and higher pressure in both groups. Comparison of correlations between blood pressure, tension and anger with the correlations of pressure with a control mood scale permitted spurious associations based on expectancies or reporting biases to be distinguished from genuine effects. Only the correlation between tension and systolic pressure in the hypertensive group exceeded the correlation with the control mood scale. Self-monitored pressure also correlated with pressure levels recorded in the laboratory. These results suggest that examination of blood pressure variations and psychological factors on a longitudinal basis may be valuable, particularly in the development of self-management procedures for essential hypertensives.

The study of psychological characteristics in essential hypertension has received fresh impetus from the development of behavioural intervention techniques. Psychological evaluations may not only help identify individuals at risk and predict responses to treatment, but may uncover elements that are amenable to direct intervention; hence the recent suggestion that cognitive behavioural methods and social skills training may be employed to modify the social competence of hypertensives (Linden & Feuerstein, 1981).

This paper concerns the relationship of essential hypertension with two aspects of psychological functioning. The first aim was to determine whether clinical status is associated with a consistent pattern of scores on measures of anxiety, hostility and Type A behaviour. The study of personality in hypertension has a long but chequered history (Steptoe, 1981). In part, this is due to the use of unstandardized ratings or subjective measures (e.g. Harris *et al.*, 1953; Safar *et al.*, 1978). However, the problems of patient selection are also responsible for many of the discrepancies between studies.

The first major difficulty is referral bias. Comparisons are frequently made between diagnosed hypertensives and controls. Yet diagnosed patients are not typical of the hypertensive population as a whole; they complain of more symptoms and have higher neuroticism scores than people with comparable blood pressure (BP) whose hypertension has not been detected (Robinson, 1964; Berglund *et al.*, 1975; Goldberg *et al.*, 1980). Moreover, antihypertensive medications may influence scores on psychological tests (Robinson, 1964).

Referral bias not only affects hypertensives but comparison subjects, who may enter the study knowing their status as controls. For example, Esler and his colleagues (1977) have reported differences on measures of hostility and suppression of anger between normotensives and mild hypertensives with high plasma renin activity. However, the normotensives were volunteers recruited by advertisement, and had not been exposed to the administrative and diagnostic procedures employed for patients.

0144-6657/82/040303 – 09 $02.00/0 © 1982 The British Psychological Society

In an effort to circumvent this problem, many investigators have used a cross-sectional screening approach, correlating BPs from unselected populations with psychological test scores. Some links with psychological disturbance are suggested in these analyses (Harburg *et al.*, 1973; Haynes *et al.*, 1978), although results are again inconsistent (see Monk, 1980). Unfortunately, a second difficulty emerges in such investigations, since BP on screening is generally higher than that recorded on subsequent occasions (Dunne, 1969); the group identified as hypertensive on screening will therefore contain a substantial proportion of false positives.

Few reports have satisfied both the requirements of selection without bias, and reliability of diagnostic status. The studies of Cochrane (1973) and Davies (1970) did fulfil these criteria, and neither showed disturbances of psychological questionnaire responses amongst hypertensives. This suggests that the personality differences identified elsewhere may have been confounded by selection factors. The present study also met methodological requirements by screening a large population, and then subjecting possible hypertensives and normotensives to identical procedures. No individual was informed of his clinical status until the end of the entire test battery, so that results were not confounded by knowledge of diagnosis. The measures included were selected as the factors most frequently linked with high blood pressure in the literature.

The second aspect of psychological function explored in this paper was the relationship of BP variation with mood within individuals. Whitehead *et al.* (1977) studied 25 hypertensive patients, who measured their own BP four times daily for several weeks, completing analogue ratings of anxiety and anger at the same time. Although correlations varied widely amongst individuals, higher BP readings were predominantly associated with negative mood. This study suggested that links between variations in BP and psychological factors might profitably be explored on a within-subject basis. Such a procedure could be particularly valuable during behavioural intervention, since patients are frequently sceptical that BP is influenced by emotional responses. Unfortunately, the general implications of the survey were limited. Patients were recruited by advertisements asking for volunteers with high BP and nervousness, so a strong selection bias was operating. Nor was there a normotensive control group. Moreover, it is possible that subjects' BP assessments were influenced by their mood, or vice versa, leading to spurious positive correlations. The recent examination of correlations between emotions, physical sensations and BP variations in normotensive students may likewise have been contaminated by expectancy effects (Pennebaker *et al.*, 1982).

Since the technique used in these investigations relies on participants recording both BP and subjective ratings, it is impossible completely to eliminate cross-referencing and bias. Nevertheless, the attempt was made in the present study to examine the association with more rigorous methodology. Rating scales and BP values were placed on the obverse sides of each diary sheet, to prevent direct comparison. A control mood scale (depression), not expected to relate to BP, was included together with tension and anger, in order to identify any recording biases; no consistent links between depression and BP have been reported either in survey or case-control studies (Wheatley *et al.*, 1975; Friedman & Bennet, 1977; Goldberg *et al.*, 1980; Monk, 1980). The magnitude of correlations between tension, anger and BP were thus compared with depression/BP, using the latter as a reporting-bias referent. Finally, associations were assessed in naïve hypertensives and normotensives recruited through screening, instead of selecting subjects already predisposed in favour of the hypothesis.

Method

Subject recruitment

Blood pressure screening was carried out over nine separate days in two factories and one large Post Office Depot. All employees who wished to have their BP taken were included, and circulars were distributed in order to encourage participation. The majority of volunteers were shop floor workers, with a small number of clerical staff. Males aged 55 or less with BP in the range of 175/110 to 145/90 (lower limit 145/95 for the 45–55 age group) were recalled for further examination. Those with a known history of hypertension or heart disease, and those currently taking medication for any complaint were not retested. Hypertensive women and men with BP exceeding the upper criterion were referred to their general practitioners. After the investigation had continued for several weeks, a series of 13 males with BP under 145/90 who matched the hypertensives in age distribution were also recruited from the screened population.

Procedure

Before screening, participants completed a brief record sheet giving details of medications, cigarette smoking, and last BP measurement. Blood pressure (diastolic phase V) was recorded from the left arm using Visomat (Boehringer) electronic sphygmomanometers, supplemented by a stethoscope where necessary, and pulse rates were recorded manually. Two BP readings were completed after three and five minutes sitting, and one or two standing. No participant was informed of possible diagnosis at the time of screening.

Possible hypertensives and normotensive controls were later sent a letter asking them to undergo further tests in the hospital. The interval between screening and hospital appointment varied from two to nine weeks owing to scheduling difficulties. On arrival at out-patients, a 12-lead electrocardiograph was recorded in the ECG Department, and blood and urine were collected for tests of plasma urea, serum electrolytes and urinalysis. These measurements were carried out in order to detect cases of secondary hypertension or heart disease. Subjects were then given a standard clinical examination (by DM), in which a full medical history was taken together with family history of cardiovascular disease. BP was again recorded after three to five minutes sitting and on standing. Subjects also filled in the Hostility and Direction of Hostility Questionnaire (HDHQ; Caine *et al.*, 1967). Total hostility scores, together with estimates of outwardly directed (extropunitive) and self-directed (intropunitive) hostility were computed.

Participants were then studied in the psychophysiological laboratory. Here they completed the state scale of the State–Trait Anxiety Inventory (STAI; Spielberger *et al.*, 1970) and a Type A questionnaire. This latter instrument, developed by Krantz *et al.* (1974) for use with students and later employed by Steptoe & Ross (1981), contains 21 scored items dealing with self-assessments of punctuality, temperament, frequency of exposure to deadlines, etc., embedded in a number of buffer items. It was adapted for use with this working population by adjustments in wording.

On completion of these questionnaires, the participant sat quietly in the laboratory while psychophysiological recordings were taken. Heart rate, pulse transit time, skin conductance level, respiration rate and tidal volume were recorded continuously using a Grass 7 polygraph, while BP was monitored every minute using the Grass pre-amplifier Model 7P8E. The last four readings from the laboratory rest session (taken after at least 15 min sitting quietly) were later scored and averaged to provide a further estimate of BP.

Before leaving the laboratory, subjects were taught to monitor their own BP, using a stethoscope and aneroid sphygmomanometer. A double stethoscope was constructed in order to ensure accurate perception of Korotkoff sounds. Patients were then given a BP self-monitoring diary. Each diary sheet had space for four estimations of BP, and suitable recording times were arranged on an individual basis. On one side of the sheet, three visual analogue scales were drawn: the extremes were labelled tense–relaxed, cheerful–depressed, angry–cool. Participants were asked to complete these ratings before taking BP, and the spaces for pressure readings were placed on the obverse. Two estimates of BP were recorded on each occasion, and the readings were averaged for subsequent analysis.

Blood pressure self-monitoring was continued for 14 days, after which subjects returned to the laboratory. Accuracy was checked by use of the double stethoscope, and corrections in the BP diaries were made if appropriate. The Trait scale of the STAI was completed, after which participants underwent a laboratory session of behavioural stress tests. The data from this session will be reported elsewhere (Steptoe *et al.*, in preparation). Normotensives and subjects whose BP had fallen during the course of these investigations were then reassured that the tests had all been favourable. Those whose BP remained elevated were referred for behavioural or pharmacological treatment.

Data analysis

Three sets of BP recordings were used to categorize groups: levels on screening, the out-patient examination (clinic BP), and measures from the end of the first laboratory session (rest session BP). Only individuals whose BP exceeded criterion on all three occasions were allocated to the mild hypertension group. Comparisons on questionnaire measures were made between these patients and normotensives using two-tailed Student t tests.

The analysis of BP self-monitoring excluded readings from day 1 in case initial unfamiliarity with the procedure influenced values. Since some patients did not complete 14 days, analysis of variance for both systolic and diastolic BP was undertaken on 12 days. In addition, a diurnal profile was constructed by averaging across the 12 days for each of the four time periods; these time periods corresponded to 7–9 a.m., 12–2 p.m., 5–7 p.m., and 9–11 p.m. Ratings on the mood scales were converted to numbers on a nine-point scale, ranging from 1 (extreme tension, depression and anger) to 9 (extreme relaxation, cheerfulness and coolness). Six product moment correlations between mood and BP were computed for each subject (systolic and diastolic BP against the three mood scales). Within each group, the z-transformed tension/BP and anger/BP correlations were compared separately with depression/BP using Student t tests. This procedure was chosen in preference to repeated measures analysis of variance, since some individuals completed only two rating scales.

Results

Survey and blood pressure data

A total of 694 men and 176 women were screened; of these, 74 men and 22 women were either recalled for further examination or referred to their general practitioners with suspected hypertension. Overall, therefore, 10·7 per cent men and 12·5 per cent women were identified as possible cases.

Thirty-five possible hypertensives and 13 normotensives were called for examination in the clinic. Two failed to complete the protocol, while one man was excluded when significant cardiac disease was discovered. Of the 32 men who completed all tests, 16 were classed as mild hypertensives on the criterion outlined earlier.

Table 1 summarizes the BP data from the two groups at each measurement period. Systolic and diastolic BPs were significantly different ($t = 4\cdot42$ to $11\cdot5$, d.f. $= 27$, $P<0\cdot001$) on all occasions. The groups did not differ on age or body weight.

Table 1. Patient characteristics

		Hypertensives (n = 16)		Normotensives (n = 13)	
		mean	(SD)	mean	(SD)
Screening	SP	148·8	(12·6)	119·4	(11·6)
	DP	98·9	(3·3)	78·7	(6·0)
Clinic	SP	145·3	(14·8)	123·1	(11·7)
	DP	93·3	(4·8)	77·2	(8·5)
Rest	SP	148·4	(13·4)	128·8	(8·7)
Session	DP	101·2	(10·9)	81·5	(7·2)
Age		45·9	(7·2)	42·4	(9·4)
Body weight (lb)		164·7	(21·4)	159·0	(15·9)

Adequate self-monitoring was achieved by 15 hypertensives and 12 normotensives. Analysis of variance of self-monitored BP confirmed group differences for systolic ($F=22\cdot9$, d.f. $= 1,25$, $P<0\cdot001$) and diastolic levels ($F=34\cdot2$, d.f. $= 1,25$, $P<0\cdot001$). The mean self-monitored BP was 152·1/100·8 and 127·5/84·0 in hypertensives and normotensives respectively; unlike some other studies, these readings are no lower than those recorded in the clinic (Laughlin *et al.*, 1980). Product moment analysis indicated that across the whole sample, rest session and mean self-monitored BP were highly correlated ($r=0\cdot668$ for systolic and 0·626 for diastolic BP, $P<0\cdot001$).

A main effect for day emerged in analysis of self-monitored systolic and diastolic BP ($F = 2\cdot51$ and $2\cdot36$, d.f. $= 11,275$, $P<0\cdot01$). Levels tended to be higher on the first day analysed (day 2 of recording), but subsequently stabilized. Analysis of diurnal variations yielded a significant effect for time period in systolic BP only ($F = 5\cdot64$, d.f. $= 3,75$, $P<0\cdot01$). Systolic BP rose progressively across samples from a mean of $138\cdot2$mm in the morning to $143\cdot5$mm in the evening.

Psychological questionnaire data

The outcome of group comparisons on psychological questionnaire responses are shown in Table 2. There were no significant differences in trait anxiety, total hostility or the two directional hostility measures. Type A scores were significantly higher in the normotensives than hypertensives; however, it should be noted that in both cases the mean levels are very low. Previous research in this laboratory and elsewhere has found means among students of 7 to 8 (Krantz *et al.*, 1974; Steptoe & Ross, 1981). The normotensives also showed significantly higher State anxiety with a mean excess of $5\cdot1$ points over hypertensives. These questionnaires did not therefore show heightened anxiety or hostility amongst hypertensives.

Table 2. Group means on personality questionnaires

	Hypertensives ($n = 16$)	Normotensives ($n = 13$)	t (d.f. $= 27$)
Type A Questionnaire	3·31	5·69	−2·09*
HDHQ −			
Total	14·31	13·2	0·52
Intropunitive	4·38	3·75	0·53
Extropunitive	9·94	9·42	0·40
STAI −			
Trait	34·1	37·0	0·92
State	29·1	34·2	−2·15*

*$P<0\cdot05$.

Mood ratings and blood pressure

Three of the hypertensives and two of the normotensives who provided adequate self-monitoring diaries failed to complete mood scales satisfactorily. Either they omitted ratings on several occasions, or endorsed only one of the three mood scales.

Self-monitored BP and mood were negatively correlated in both groups. The median correlation coefficient was negative in all six comparisons amongst hypertensives and in five out of six in normotensives. Thus higher BP tended to be associated with ratings of greater tension and anger. Since higher BP also correlated with negative mood on the control scale (depression), a reporting bias in favour of the hypothesized pattern may have been operating.

Accordingly, correlations between BP and anger or tension were compared with the BP/depression correlation. These analyses yielded only one significant effect: the negative correlation between systolic BP and tension − relaxation in hypertensives was significantly higher (mean $z = -0\cdot107$) than the correlation between systolic BP and depression ($z = -0\cdot013$; $t = 2\cdot28$, d.f. $= 11$, $P<0\cdot05$). None of the correlations between BP and anger or tension in normotensives, or between diastolic BP and mood in hypertensives, exceeded the levels recorded on the reference variable. The data thus provide limited support for a link between mood and BP, but only for systolic BP against self-reported tension − relaxation in hypertensives.

Blood pressure variability

The fact that significant links between mood and BP emerged only in hypertensives may be due to heightened pressure variability in this group. Comparisons were therefore made between normotensives and hypertensives in the range of self-monitored BP.

Two indices of range were computed: the maximum difference between daily averages of BP (between-day range), and the maximum difference between the time periods averaged across days (diurnal range). The mean range scores are summarized in Table 3; and since none of the differences between groups was significant, there was no evidence for greater within-subject variability in self-monitored BP amongst hypertensives.

Table 3. Mean ranges of self-monitored BP (mm Hg)

	Hypertensive ($n = 15$)	Normotensive ($n = 12$)
Between-day range		
SP	6·32	6·15
DP	4·08	4·27
Diurnal range		
SP	6·24	5·31
DP	5·08	2·46

Correlations of variability against BP level ($n = 27$)

	Between-day range		Diurnal range	
	SP	DP	SP	DP
Rest session				
SP	0·298	0·085	0·425*	0·499**
DP	0·444*	0·444*	0·241	0·253

*$P<0·05$; **$P<0·01$.

Nevertheless, across the whole cohort, interesting patterns of self-monitored BP variability were revealed with correlational analyses. These are tabulated in Table 3. Systolic BP levels registered during rest session correlated significantly with diurnal BP range, while rest session diastolic BP levels correlated with the between day range. This suggests that individuals with higher pressures in the rest session also showed greater variability in their self-monitored BP.

Discussion

Our results underline the prevalence and serious nature of high BP. Out of the total screened sample, one in 10 men and women were re-examined or referred for possible hypertension. None of these had any history of cardiovascular disease, and many could not recall having their BP recorded for more than 20 years. Although a proportion of these suspected hypertensives were cleared on follow-up, a number exhibited signs of disease requiring urgent treatment.

The problems of patient selection outlined in the introduction are illustrated in the results of the present survey. In order to overcome the biases of referral, medical history and knowledge of diagnosis, many studies categorize patients on the basis of BP recorded on a single occasion. However, the lability of BP makes divisions on this basis dubious. Fifty per cent of the men re-examined as suspected hypertensives in the present study were excluded after repeated measurement. The pattern of psychological test data may therefore be confounded if patients are assigned to groups on one BP measure alone.

On the other hand, detailed cardiovascular and psychological evaluation is seldom performed without informing hypertensives (and controls) of their clinical status. The solution adopted in the present study was not to inform any participant of his possible diagnosis on screening. Our calls for further testing were couched in vague but reassuring terms in order to alleviate any unnecessary concern amongst normotensive controls. It was thus possible to compare well-defined hypertensives with adequate controls from the same population.

This study focused on patients with mild hypertension, rather than more severe groups. Investigations of the mechanisms underlying hypertension suggest that autonomic factors are likely to be most important at this stage (Julius & Esler, 1975; Steptoe, 1981). In established hypertension, renal and vascular processes are more prominent in maintaining the haemodynamic disturbance. Thus if psychological factors are of any significance in the aetiology of hypertension (rather than reaction to the disorder), they will be identified in patients at an early phase.

However, our comparison between hypertensives and normotensives revealed few differences on standard psychological tests. The HDHQ was administered since hostility has repeatedly been implicated in the literature. Portions of the test were also used by Mann (1977), who observed significant differences on two of the questionnaires subscales. Unfortunately, Mann administered the HDHQ after participants knew their status as hypertensive or normotensive in the study. The present negative result is consistent with Cochrane (1973), who also collected data through population screening.

Significantly higher state anxiety was recorded from normotensives, although trait anxiety did not distinguish the groups. The explanation for this effect is not clear, although a similar pattern was observed by Davies (1970) in another study of male factory workers. Another significant difference emerged in response to the Type A questionnaire. This result must be interpreted with caution, since the inventory is in many ways inappropriate for shop floor workers. It includes items concerning work deadlines and work during vacations and weekends that do not apply to this population. Thus scores in both groups are low. Nonetheless, the observation of low Type A scores amongst people with high BP is consistent with results previously obtained from student populations in this laboratory (Steptoe & Ross, 1981). Large scale epidemiological studies have also shown little relationship between BP level and Type A scores (Shekelle *et al.*, 1976).

The paucity of factors distinguishing groups suggests that differences reported elsewhere in the literature may have been due to selection of atypical hypertensives. Our results are similar to those of Davies (1970) and Cochrane (1973), who also identified hypertensives through repeated measurements on screened populations. An alternative strategy for examining psychological aspects of this condition is through longitudinal within-subject investigations. The correlational results on mood and BP offer preliminary support for this approach. These data also provide partial confirmation of the effects reported by Whitehead *et al.* (1977). As in that study, a wide range of correlations was observed between individuals, with correlation coefficients as high as -0.65 in some subjects. However, these patterns may have emerged through bias in self-monitoring and mood ratings. In comparison with correlations on the control mood scale, only one reliable difference emerged (tension/relaxation and systolic BP in hypertensives). Even in this case the mean z was only -0.107, so the association is a modest one. It did not appear to be accounted for by heightened variability in self-monitored systolic BP amongst hypertensives. These results indicate that the covariation of self-reported anger and BP observed by Whitehead *et al.* (1977) may have been spurious.

The association between BP variability (range scores) and rest session BP is interesting. A similar effect was reported by Julius *et al.* (1974), but has not been found in more recent studies (Laughlin *et al.*, 1980; Engel *et al.*, 1981). However, the later investigators did not include normotensive control groups in their evaluations. Furthermore, Engel *et al.* (1981) failed to check the reliability of self-monitored BP after the technique was first learned. Their 'professional' BPs were also recorded in an unstandardized fashion by a number of different nurses and physicians, and reliability was again not determined.

The use of self-monitoring permits fine-grained explorations not only of BP covariations with mood but concurrent behaviour. Longitudinal within-subject analyses may help patients identify circumstances that are associated with high BP episodes, while demonstrating the links between emotions, activities and cardiovascular function. This approach is now being applied in behavioural treatment research, as a preliminary to stress management (Kallinke *et al.*, in press). The method is thus potentially valuable not only in aetiological but intervention research on high blood pressure.

Acknowledgements

This project was supported by the Medical Research Council, UK. The authors are grateful for the cooperation of the staff and management of J. E. Hanger & Co. Ltd, Smiths Meters Ltd, and the General Post Office (Battersea District).

References

Berglund, G., Ander, S., Lindström, B. & Tibblin, G. (1975). Personality and reporting of symptoms in normotensive and hypertensive 50 year old males. *Journal of Psychosomatic Research,* 19, 139–145.

Caine, T. M., Foulds, G. A. & Hope, K. (1967). *Manual of the Hostility and Direction of Hostility Questionnaire.* London: University of London Press.

Cochrane, R. (1973). Hostility and neuroticism among unselected essential hypertensives. *Journal of Psychosomatic Research,* 17, 215–218.

Davies, M. (1970). Blood pressure and personality. *Journal of Psychosomatic Research,* 14, 89–104.

Dunne, J. F. (1969). Variation of blood pressure in untreated hypertensive outpatients. *Lancet,* i, 391–392.

Engel, B. T., Gaarder, K. R. & Glasgow, M. (1981). Behavioral treatment of high blood pressure I. Analyses of intra- and interdaily variations of blood pressure during a one-month, baseline period. *Psychosomatic Medicine,* 43, 255–270.

Esler, M., Julius, S., Zweifler, A., Randall, O., Harburg, E., Gardiner, H. & DeQuattro, V. (1977). Mild high-renin essential hypertension: A neurogenic human hypertension? *New England Journal of Medicine,* 296, 405–411.

Friedman, M. J. & Bennet, P. L. (1977). Depression and hypertension. *Psychosomatic Medicine,* 39, 134–142.

Goldberg, E. L., Comstock, G. W. & Graves, C. G. (1980). Psychosocial factors and blood pressure. *Psychological Medicine,* 10, 243–255.

Harburg, E., Erfurt, J. C., Hauenstein, L. S., Chape, C., Schull, W. J. & Schork, M. A. (1973). Socio-ecological stress, suppressed hostility, skin color, and black–white male blood pressure: Detroit. *Psychosomatic Medicine,* 35, 276–296.

Harris, R. E., Sokolow, M., Carpenter, L. G., Freedman, M. & Hunt, S. P. (1953). Response to psychologic stress in persons who are potentially hypertensive. *Circulation,* 7, 874–879.

Haynes, S. G., Levine, S., Scotch, N., Feinleib, M. & Kannel, W. B. (1978). The relationship of psychosocial factors to coronary heart disease in the Framingham study. I. Methods and risk factors. *American Journal of Epidemiology,* 107, 362–383.

Julius, S., Ellis, C. N., Pascual, A. V., Matice, M., Hansson, L., Hunyar, S. N. & Sandler, L. N. (1974). Home blood pressure determination. Value in borderline ('labile') hypertension. *Journal of the American Medical Association,* 229, 663–666.

Julius, S. & Esler, M. D. (1975). Autonomic nervous cardiovascular regulation in borderline hypertension. *American Journal of Cardiology,* 36, 685–696.

Kallinke, D., Kulick, B. & Heim, P. (in press). Behaviour analysis and treatment of essential hypertensives. *Journal of Psychosomatic Research.*

Krantz, D. S., Glass, D. C. & Snyder, M. L. (1974). Helplessness, stress level and the coronary-prone behavior pattern. *Journal of Abnormal Psychology,* 10, 284–300.

Laughlin, K. D., Sherrard, D. J. & Fisher, L. (1980). Comparison of clinic and home blood pressure levels in essential hypertension and variables associated with clinic–home differences. *Journal of Chronic Disease,* 33, 197–206.

Linden, W. & Feuerstein, M. (1981). Essential hypertension and social coping behaviour. *Journal of Human Stress,* 7(1), 28–34.

Mann, A. H. (1977). Psychiatric morbidity and hostility in hypertension. *Psychological Medicine,* 7, 653–659.

Monk, M. (1980). Psychologic status and hypertension. *American Journal of Epidemiology,* 112, 200–208.

Pennebaker, J. W., Gonder-Frederick, L., Stewart, H., Elfman, L. & Skelton, J. A. (1982). Physical symptoms associated with blood pressure. *Psychophysiology,* 19, 201–210.

Robinson, B. F. (1964). A possible effect of selection on the test scores of a group of hypertensives. *Journal of Psychosomatic Research,* **8**, 239–243.

Safar, M. E., Kamieniecka, H. A., Levenson, J. A., Dimitriu, V. M. & Pauleau, N. F. (1978). Haemodynamic factors and Rorschach testing in borderline and sustained hypertension. *Psychosomatic Medicine,* **40**, 620–630.

Shekelle, R. B., Schoenberger, J. A. & Stamler, J. (1976). Correlates of the JAS Type A behavior score. *Journal of Chronic Disease,* **29**, 381–394.

Speilberger, C. D., Gorsuch, R. L. & Lushene, R. E. (1970). *STAI Manual.* Palo Alto, CA: Consulting Psychologists Press.

Steptoe, A. (1981). *Psychological Factors in Cardiovascular Disorders.* London: Academic Press.

Steptoe, A., Melville, D. & Ross, A. (in preparation). Behavioural response demands, cardiovascular reactivity and essential hypertension.

Steptoe, A. & Ross, A. (1981). Psychophysiological reactivity and the prediction of cardiovascular disorders. *Journal of Psychosomatic Research,* **25**, 23–32.

Wheatley, D., Balter, M., Levine, J., Lipman, R., Bauer, M. L. & Bonato, R. (1975). Psychiatric aspects of hypertension. *British Journal of Psychiatry,* **127**, 327–336.

Whitehead, W. E., Blackwell, B., DeSilva, H. & Robinson, A. (1977). Anxiety and anger in hypertension. *Journal of Psychosomatic Research,* **21**, 383–389.

Received 20 April 1982

Requests for reprints should be addressed to Dr Andrew Steptoe, Department of Psychology, St George's Hospital Medical School, Cranmer Terrace, Tooting, London SW17, UK.

British Journal of Clinical Psychology (1982), **21**, 313–320   *Printed in Great Britain*

A behavioural perspective on chronic pain

Wilbert E. Fordyce

This review outlines a behavioural view of chronic pain, in which pain behaviours are considered as operants. This view is supported by experiments in which pain behaviour is shown to be under the influence of environmental factors. The number of exercises performed by pain patients working to tolerance tend to be in multiples of five, rather than following a chance distribution. The exercise deficit seen in pain patients under conditions where exercises are counted does not occur when feedback is removed, and under these circumstances pain patients do not differ from normals. Other studies show that tolerance can be increased by verbal reinforcement, and that pain ratings are influenced by the presence or absence of a patient's spouse. Implications of these findings for the maintenance or reduction of chronic pain are discussed.

At the outset, it is important to distinguish acute or recent onset from chronic pain. It is equally important to distinguish trauma-induced pain from pain relating to some ongoing disease process, e.g. cancer, rheumatoid arthritis. The focus of this paper is on trauma-induced pain which has persisted past expected healing time and is therefore appropriately considered as chronic. While, as will be seen from the paper by Redd (this issue, pp. 351–358), the concepts and methods discussed here may have relevance to other pain or chronic illness problems, and perhaps to some aspects of acute pain, the central focus is on trauma-induced chronic pain.

The incidence and prevalence of chronic low back pain is great. In the United States, 56 per cent of the labour force (Snook, 1980) will ultimately receive treatment for back pain. Chronic low back pain, in industrial settings, makes up the single most expensive medical insurance cost factor. Approximately 4 per cent of the claimants for wage replacement funding and health care services are for low back pain but they account for 36 per cent of annual expenditures for all disability categories (Johnson, 1978). Those and numerous other studies attest to the magnitude of the problem.

The persistence of back pain in the face of numerous diagnostic and treatment procedures is itself an index of limitations of traditional methods.

Pain tends to be viewed by the health care system in disease model terms. The assumption is made that indicators of pain (symptoms) occur as a consequence of the antecedent stimulus of nociception, i.e. stimulation of peripheral nerve endings from body damage. Diagnosis seeks to identify the body damage evoking pain; treatment seeks to eliminate or reduce it. When treatment fails to restore full function and/or the pain persists, typically the patient is cycled and recycled through diagnostic or treatment regimens based on the same conceptual model. If the model does not lead to a solution, perhaps the problem is with the model. The physician and other health care purveyors have an implicit commitment to do *something* about the patient's pain problem but are faced with the limitations of the disease model, aggravated by the persistent endorsement of that model by any number of professional colleagues. An alternative way of looking at chronic pain, and other chronic illness, is proposed.

Loeser (1980) proposes a different way of conceptualizing the domain of pain. In relation to a problem of chronic pain, and the person who has it, the data are the person's communications by word or deed that there is suffering with what is labelled as 'pain', augmented by whatever historical or currently observed 'physical findings' appear to have potential causal relationships to those communications of suffering. The communications of suffering are not 'pain'. They are a set of behaviours to which we, observer and sufferer,

0144-6657/82/040313–08 $02.00/0 © 1982 The British Psychological Society assign the term, 'pain'. Loeser proposes we recognize distinctions among nociception, pain, suffering, and pain behaviour. Briefly, these terms are defined as:

Nociception: Potential tissue damaging thermal or mechanical energy impinging upon specialized nerve endings of A-delta and C fibres.

Pain: Perceived nociceptive input to the nervous system.

Suffering: Negative affective response generated in higher nervous centres by pain and other situations: loss of loved objects, stress, anxiety, etc.

Pain behaviour: All forms of behaviour generated by the individual commonly understood to reflect the presence of nociception, including speech, facial expression, posture, taking medicines, seeking health care intervention, refusing to work.

There are a number of key points to recognize about these definitions. First, there is no inherent link between nociception and pain. There can be pain without nociception, as in some central pain states (e.g. Tic Douloureux, phantom limb pain, post-herpetic neuralgia). There can also be nociception without pain, as when hypnosis provides total analgesia for a surgical procedure, or when a combat soldier is wounded and is unaware of that wound for several hours. Secondly, it is well understood that how we label events will influence how we perceive them; for example, when we use the language of pain to label suffering. We may say that a person gives us a 'pain in the neck'. We do not mean there is nociception in the neck, or even that our neck 'hurts'. We mean the person causes us to suffer. Again, we may speak of the 'pain' we experience at the loss of a dear one. We do not mean there is nociception or pain in some part of our bodies. We mean the loss causes us to suffer, but use the language of pain to communicate that suffering. Thus, language styles lead us toward confounding suffering and pain and the labelling of our suffering influences how we perceive it. Thirdly, pain behaviours, whether they be word or action, *are* behaviour. As such, they are subject to the same influences as other kinds of behaviour. Finally, when we observe a pain patient, it is behaviour that we are observing. The critical question in diagnosis must always be, 'why do those pain behaviours occur?' It is improper to restrict the question to: 'What nociception "causes" those pain behaviours?'

Conceptual basis for viewing pain behaviour in behavioural terms

The redundancy in the heading to this paragraph was deliberate, for it reminds us that pain behaviours are behaviour. More precisely, pain behaviours are operants. Skinner (1953) called our attention many years ago to the distinction between respondents and operants. Respondents, involving smooth muscle or glandular actions, are essentially reflexive. This is another way of stating that they are controlled by antecedent stimuli. Given an adequate stimulus in an intact organism, the response occurs. Operants, in contrast, involve striated or voluntary musclature. They may be elicited by antecedent stimuli, as in the operant withdrawal response of removing the hand from a hot stove. Operants, however, have the critically important characteristic of being sensitive to consequences. Immediate or anticipated reinforcing consequences can and do exert influence on the probable future occurrence of a given operant. We need not concern ourselves here with the details of the factors which influence reinforcement effects, such as the frequency and timing of reinforcement, and determination of what in fact will or will not be reinforcing. For the purposes of this paper, it is enough to recognize that pain behaviours are operants. As such, they are sensitive to learning/conditioning effects through contingent reinforcement.

Conceptually, pain behaviour might be said to occur for either or both of two reasons. One is a response to a nociceptive antecedent stimulus. In such an instance, the pain problem or pain behaviours might be said to be respondent in character. Alternatively, pain behaviours may occur because of conditioning effects, i.e. because of reinforcing contingencies to which they lead or to which they are anticipated to lead by the suffering person. In that event, the pain problem or pain behaviours might be said to be operant in character.

In the practical case, the process can be characterized as one in which pain behaviours originate as a consequence of body injury which produces nociception. If, however, those pain behaviours persist, for whatever reason, and do so in an environment productive of conditioning effects, in time the pain behaviours may continue long past healing time for reasons quite different from those eliciting them at the time of injury. Extant conditioning effects or prior conditioning experiences may exert influence sufficient to bring the pain behaviours under 'social' control, i.e. under control of factors outside the person in the form of reinforcing consequences contingent on pain behaviours.

It should be noted that the behavioural or learning/conditioning model described here is distinctly different from traditional psychodynamic models. In those models, such terms as psychogenic, conversion reaction, hysteria, etc., are invoked in an attempt to explain the discrepancy between pain behaviours and physical findings. Such approaches, like the disease model perspective, seek 'explanations' within the person. They fail to come to grips systematically with conditioning effects linked to environmental cues and consequences. They also have failed empirically to provide solutions or treatment methods successful for problems of chronic pain.

Data basis for viewing pain behaviour as influenced by environmental contingencies

There have by now been published a series of papers reporting favourable outcomes when chronic pain is treated by behavioural or some mix of cognitive/behavioural methods (e.g Fordyce *et al.*, 1973; Greenhoot & Sternbach, 1974; Gottlieb *et al.*, 1977; Newman *et al.*, 1978; Swanson *et al.*, 1979; Block *et al.*, 1980; Roberts & Rheinhardt, 1980). No attempt will be made here to review those. Rather, a more focal approach to a data base will be presented. Four studies will be described which are taken to support the thesis that pain behaviours may be influenced systematically by factors in the environment.

First, a study by Fordyce *et al.* (1979) addressed the question of the meaning of a patient reporting he/she can do no more of a prescribed exercise because of 'pain'. A series of 77 chronic pain patients, all in treatment and all doing prescribed physical therapy exercises, were studied. The therapist instructions to each patient were to perform the prescribed exercise '... until pain, weakness, or fatigue cause you to want to stop. You decide when to stop' (work-to-tolerance). The question asked of the data concerned the number on which patients stopped. *A priori*, for a given person and a given exercise, there should be an approximate equal probability for any number of repetitions of an exercise. There were a total of 442 occasions from these 77 patients in which the number of repetitions of an exercise was recorded. Repetitions were grouped according to the last digit, i.e. 11, 21, 31, etc., and 16, 26, 36, etc. These values were then further grouped into the 1−6 cluster; 12, 22, 32, etc., and 17, 27, 37, etc., into the 2−7 cluster, and so on. Figure 1 shows the results. It will be observed that subjects stopped on a multiple of 5 (i.e. 5, 10, 15, 20, 25, etc.) approximately 50 per cent of the time. Had the pain behaviour of ceasing exercise occurred because tolerance had been reached, the distribution of last digit frequencies should have approximated chance, a level shown by the dotted line across Fig. 1.

A second study was carried out by the same experimenters. Chronic pain patients under evaluation and not yet in treatment were compared with a control group of non-patients, all of whom reported no pain problems. Subjects exercised to tolerance on apparatus designed to minimize or obfuscate information about how much work had been done. A total of 11 exercise set-ups were arranged; two of which will be described to illustrate the process. A fixed bicycle was provided which had no speed or distance indicator. In addition, by means of linkage to electronically operated equipment, the gear ratio was changed each few seconds on a variable schedule. Asynchronously, the drag on the axle also increased or decreased by variable amounts each few seconds. As a second example, a metal rod was suspended by cables some 18 inches above a plinth. The cables in turn were connected to weights suspended out of sight of the subject who reclined on the plinth. A light was suspended from the ceiling above his head. Again by means of electronic equipment, the light and the metal rod and attached weights were controlled on a variable schedule. Instructions were to push against the rod to keep the light turned on. As the amount of weight linked to the rod varied, greater or lesser amounts of force were required. The intervals at a given weight of resistance against which the subject pushed, varied across a range of a few seconds. The effect was to make it impossible to keep precise track of how much effort had been required to keep the light on.

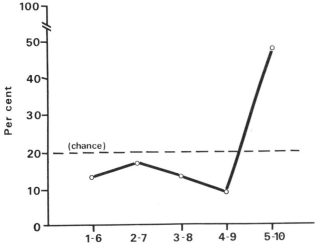

Figure 1. Exercise tolerance values.

In this second study, the only method by which performance could be measured was for each exercise distance into the electronic programme controlling the apparatus. Subjects exercised one session a day for four consecutive days. Performance the first day was given the arbitrary value of 1 and performance on each subsequent session was calculated as a ratio of that. The results are shown in Fig. 2. It is apparent from Fig. 2 first that there are

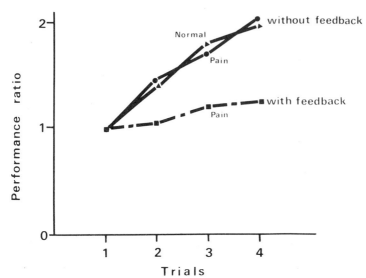

Figure 2. Exercise tolerance with and without feedback.

no differences between the chronic pain patients and controls; second that both groups consistently increased performance across sessions, such that by the fourth session they were doing approximately twice as much as in the first session. Figure 2 also shows a performance curve across four exercise sessions of a separate sample of chronic pain patients exercising to tolerance but on exercises in which they could count the repetitions of exercise performed before they decided tolerance had been reached. Their collective performance curve was plotted by calculating the ratio between the first and each subsequent session. As can be seen in Fig. 2, that curve is distinctly different; i.e. almost flat. The data from these two studies show that exercise 'tolerance' in these separate groups of chronic pain patients consistently depends on the influence of factors other than simple nociception or some other inner body cue.

Two additional studies illustrate more pointedly the impact of social feedback on what patients say about the severity of their pain, and how much exercise they in fact do when allegedly exercising to tolerance. Block *et al.* (1980) divided a group of chronic pain patients into those for whom the data indicated their spouses acted in supportive ways when pain behaviours were emitted and those for whom spouse reactions could be characterized as non-supportive. Each patient went through a 20 min structured interview in a room with a one-way mirror. Each subject was told, correctly, that his/her spouse was observing through the one-way mirror during 10 min of the interview and that the spouse was absent but a health care professional was observing during the other 10 min segment. Sequence effects were controlled by balancing. At the mid-point of each 10 min interview segment, subjects were asked to rate their present pain level on a 0–10 scale, with 0 indicating absence of pain and 10 indicating unbearable pain. Results of those pain ratings are shown in Fig. 3. Results indicate a significant interaction between spouse presence/absence and spouse supportive/non-supportive. Patients with supportive spouses rated pain higher when the spouse was observing and lower when the spouse was gone. Patients with non-supportive spouses rated pain lower when the spouse was observing and higher when the spouse was absent.

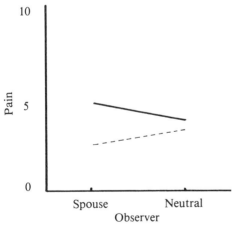

Figure 3. Present pain (after Block *et al.*, 1980). ————, spouse supportive; – – – – –, spouse non-supportive. (Reproduced with permission.)

Cairns & Pasino (1977) systematically varied physical therapist performance feedback response in a series of nine chronic pain patients exercising to tolerance. Figure 4 displays results with one of the nine subjects. The other subjects yielded comparable results. First, a base-line was established. Then performance on one exercise, riding the fixed bicycle, received systematic praise and reinforcement (VR or verbal reinforcement) contingent upon increments, while a second exercise, walking laps of fixed distance, did not. Next, a reversal was instituted. Bicycle riding performance was responded to in a neutral, nondemonstrative fashion; walking laps received praise for increments. Finally, verbal reinforcement was withdrawn from the walking, as well. As shown in Fig. 4, patient performance varied markedly and systematically according to whether the physical therapist was delivering praise.

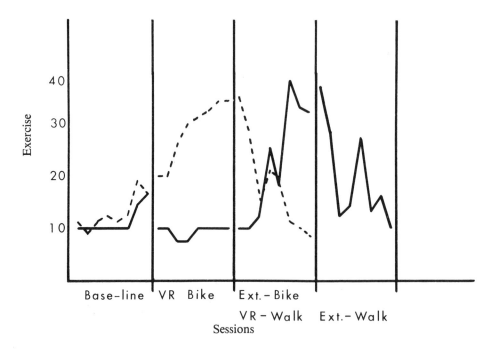

Figure 4. Effect of verbal reinforcement on exercise in chronic pain (after Cairns & Pasino, 1977). – – – – –, bike; ———, walk. (Reproduced with permission.)

These various studies in different ways all support the hypothesis that environmental factors were exerting systematic influence on exercise performance under the constant instruction to exercise to tolerance.

How conditioning may influence pain behaviours

The conceptualization presented here is that contingent reinforcement may influence pain behaviours in either of two ways, the second of which may also be divided into two subcategories. First, when pain behaviours are emitted, they may be followed in a contingent fashion by reinforcing consequences. While there are many possible examples, three should suffice to illustrate. Analgesics have traditionally been prescribed on a *prn* or take only as needed basis. The patient must indicate a need for medication before its consumption is sanctioned. That means the analgesic is pain behaviour contingent, i.e. the person must communicate suffering in order to receive the medication. If the effects of the analgesic are of positive reinforcing value for that person, a conditioning arrangement has been set up by the *prn* regimen which could be expected to strengthen the probability the person will continue to ask for analgesics.

A second example concerns rest/exercise. Pain patients typically are instructed to 'let pain be your guide' in determining when to stop an activity when 'pain' arises. If one does something and there is no pain, one can continue. If an activity leads to pain, at some point, following onset or increase of pain, one should stop. The exercising-to-tolerance mode lets rest be pain behaviour contingent. The basis for beginning rest is to emit pain behaviours. If rest is reinforcing for the person, a conditioning arrangement has been set up which may serve to strengthen pain behavioiur.

A third example concerns attention or social feedback. This has already been amply illustrated in the studies by Block *et al.* (1980) and Cairns & Pasino (1977) described above. It should suffice to add only that it is commonly the case that those around the person who emits pain behaviours often respond in ways different from those occurring in response to non-pain behaviours. If the responses to pain behaviours have special reinforcing value to the suffering person, they may serve to promote perpetuation of pain behaviours.

In addition to direct positive reinforcement of pain behaviours, conditioning would appear to play a strong role in maintenance of pain behaviours through avoidance learning effects. Avoidance learning refers to behaviours which serve either to escape a noxious stimulus, as when one withdraws a hand from a hot stove, or to avoid or postpone a noxious stimulus, as when one inhibits placing the hand on the hot stove. It has long been recognized that avoidance behaviours, once established, are difficult to extinguish. Little ongoing reinforcement is required to maintain them.

One form of avoidance learning which appears to play a major role in many chronic pain problems corresponds approximately to the traditional psychodynamic concept of secondary gain. The point can be paraphrased as, 'When I hurt (emit pain behaviours) "bad" (i.e. noxious) events do not happen which otherwise would'. One simple and common example should suffice. A person with an aversive job earns relief by spending the day resting on the divan, not only from activity/exercise, but also from the aversive events anticipated to have occurred had he/she gone to work. Put another way, the person, by spending the day on the divan earns 'time out' from an aversive job. Countless other examples are readily found.

A second way in which avoidance learning can enter in may also be explained in terms of conditioned aversive stimuli. Events associated with aversive stimuli may themselves take on aversive properties, an example of generalization of avoidance learning. Persons with long-standing pain problems may, for example, learn that doing a certain amount of an activity (e.g. walking 500 metres), leads to an increase in pain. Subsequently, when walking, they may begin to experience 'pain' on approaching the 500 metre mark either because cues in the environment have taken on the capability of eliciting the suffering response or because the person, on the basis of prior experience, anticipates that to continue past 500 metres will lead to aversive consequences, though that may no longer be true. Stated another way, it may be the case in some instances of chronic pain that the person superstitiously overguards because he/she incorrectly anticipates that the aversive consequence of increased pain which occurred earlier will occur again. Alternatively, through conditioning, environmental cues can now directly elicit the pain behaviour.

Implications for behavioural science

Much work remains to be done to explicate more precisely which persons, and under which conditions, will manifest greater or lesser amounts of what here we have termed operant pain, i.e. pain behaviours which have come under control of conditioning effects. Similarly, much work remains to be done to explicate which of the several multimodal and behaviourally based treatment tactics have the greater impact on which patients. If, however, one accepts the explanatory framework presented here, there are a number of other implications.

Perhaps of the greater importance is the recognition that many people who are suffering from chronic pain need not do so, or may be helped to suffer significantly less, by evaluative and treatment strategies which move beyond the narrow disease model perspective and take into account conditioning effects.

A second implication is that there needs to be an interactive and symbiotic relationship between medical science and behavioural science in the evaluation and management of chronic pain. Neither can do the job without the other. This in turn means a significant shift in the organization of health care delivery, as it pertains to chronic pain, from a rather exclusively 'medicalized' system to one in which behavioural as well as medical concepts and methods are brought to bear.

Finally, it would appear evident that these same points can be made about virtually any chronic illness, disease or disability. Once illness-related behaviours begin to occur, like pain behaviours, they are potentially influenced by conditioning effects. Health care delivery needs to incorporate behavioural science.

Acknowledgement

The work described in this paper was supported by Research Grant No. G008003029 from the National Institute of Handicapped Research, Department of Education, Washington, DC 20202.

References

Block, A. R., Kramer, E. F. & Gaylor, M. (1980). Behavioral treatment of chronic pain: The spouse as a discriminative cue for pain behavior. *Pain, 9*, 243–252.

Cairns, D. & Pasino, J. (1977). Comparison of verbal reinforcement and feedback in the operant treatment of disability due to chronic low back pain. *Behavior Therapy, 8*, 621–630.

Fordyce, W. E., Fowler, R. S., Lehmann, J. F., de Lateur, B. J., Sand, P. L. & Trieschmann, R. (1973). Operant conditioning in the treatment of chronic pain. *Archives of Physical Medicine and Rehabilitation, 54*, (9), 399–408.

Fordyce, W., Caldwell, L. & Hongadarom, T. (1979). Effects of performance feedback on exercise tolerance in chronic pain. Unpublished manuscript, University of Washington.

Gottlieb, H., Strite, L. D., Koller, J., Madorsky, A., Hockersmith, V., Kleeman, M. & Wagner, J. (1977). Comprehensive rehabilitation of patients having chronic low back pain. *Archives of Physical Medicine and Rehabilitation, 58*, 101–108.

Greenhoot, J. & Sternbach, R. (1974). Conjoint treatment of chronic pain. In J. Bonica (ed.), *Advances in Neurology.* vol. 4: *International symposium on pain,* pp. 595–604. New York: Raven Press.

Johnson, A. D. (1978). The problem claim: An approach to early identification. Department of Labor and Industries, State of Washington, (Mimeo).

Loeser, J. D. (1980). Perspectives on pain. *Proceedings of the First World Conference on Clinical Pharmacology and Therapeutics,* pp. 313–316. London: Macmillan.

Newman, R., Seres, J., Yospe, L. & Garlington, B. (1978). Multidisciplinary treatment of chronic pain: Long-term follow-up of low back pain patients. *Pain, 4*, 595–603.

Redd, W. H. (1982). Behavioural analysis and control of psychosomatic symptoms of patients receiving intensive cancer treatment. *British Journal of Clinical Psychology, 21*, 351–358.

Roberts, A. & Reinhardt, L. (1980). The behavioral management of chronic pain: Long term follow-up with comparison groups. *Pain, 8* (2).

Skinner, B. F. (1953). *Science and Human Behavior.* New York: Macmillan.

Snook, S. H. (1980). Low back pain in industry. Workshop on Idiopathic Low Back Pain, Miami Beach, Florida 8–10 Dec. Sponsored by (NIAMDD) American Academy of Orthopaedic Surgeons, Orthopaedic Research Society.

Swanson, D., Maruta, T. & Swenson, W. (1979). Results of behavior modification in the treatment of chronic pain. *Psychosomatic Medicine, 41*, 55–61.

Received 1 March 1982

Requests for reprints should be addressed to Professor Wilbert E. Fordyce, Rehabilitation Medicine and the Pain Service, University of Washington School of Medicine, Seattle, WA 98195, USA.

British Journal of Clinical Psychology (1982), **21**, 321 – 337   *Printed in Great Britain*

A critial review of behavioural treatments for chronic benign pain other than headache

Steven James Linton

Studies of the effectiveness of operant, relaxation, cognitive, and multimodal behavioural approaches to the treatment of chronic benign pain other than headache were evaluated. In general, the quality of the studies was poor, and most investigations lacked appropriate and adequate control conditions, outcome measures, and/or follow-ups. While outcome reports for all four behavioural treatments have been mainly positive, few data were found which conclusively demonstrate that any of the approaches are effective or that they are the treatment of choice. The data do, however, imply that behavioural approaches may help patients lead more normal and productive lives. Specifically, the literature suggests that: (1) the operant method leads to increased activity levels and decreased pain and drug intake, (2) the relaxation approach results in decreased EMG levels and some pain reductions, (3) the cognitive techniques are speculative at this time, and (4) the multimodal method regularly produces a variety of improvements, but the diversity of the treatments makes general statements about utility impossible. It is concluded that behavioural treatments for pain are warranted in the clinic and that research dealing with effectiveness and subsequently with component analyses of treatments is badly needed.

Chronic pain is a problem of considerable proportion. Yet despite considerable efforts, medical treatments often fail to relieve the pain. Patients with chronic pain usually become 'problems' in the health care system and psychological consultation may be requested. To meet this demand several behavioural treatments for chronic pain have been developed over the past 10 years. Initially these treatments were met with enthusiasm and early results were termed 'promising'. The purpose of this paper is to critically review outcome studies to evaluate whether, after roughly a decade of use, these 'promising' techniques have indeed been shown to be effective.

The most comprehensive previous review of this literature is that of Turner & Chapman (1982). While their review is generally commendable, they have only 45 per cent of the studies included in the present review which specifically deal with chronic pain other than headache. Furthermore, Turner & Chapman's inclusion of headaches in their review tends, by sheer quantity, to overshadow the results obtained with other types of chronic pain. These other pain syndromes are important since they seem to account for the majority of a pain clinic's patients. Shealy & Shealy (1976) report, for instance, that about 75 per cent of their pain clinic patients suffer from low back pain. On the other hand, headaches have been reported to account for only about 6 to 8 per cent of a pain clinic's clientele (Wang *et al.*, 1980; Arakawa, 1981) and results from the treatment of headaches may not generalize to other pain syndromes. As a result of the above considerations, an exhaustive review of behavioural treatments of chronic pain states other than headache was deemed merited.

The studies were divided into four general types of behavioural treatments for pain: operant, relaxation, cognitive, and multimodal. Categorization was based on the treatment of focus in each report. Investigations which gave equal stress to two or more treatment methods are included in the multimodal section, while articles that focused on one technique, but which used some other secondary treatment are classified according to the primary treatment. Cross-referencing is provided for studies that used techniques falling into two or more categories.

A word about chronic pain is in order before examining the outcome studies. Chronic pain usually refers to the persistent complaint of pain over at least a six-month period,

0144-6657/82/040321 – 17 $02.00/0 © 1982 The British Psychological Society

although most patients have suffered much longer. Pain is also a subjective experience, and this makes it quite difficult to measure accurately. Pain ratings, for instance, may vary between two persons or even between two time points for the same person, even though the stimulus intensity is exactly the same. Therefore, the position taken in this paper is that pain is a *set of behaviours* with such behaviours as medication intake, activity levels, mood, and pain ratings all being important components. Stress is placed on broad measures of behavioural, physiological, and cognitive or subjective aspects of pain.

The operant approach

From the operant viewpoint, pain is a set of overt responses (e.g. medication taking, limping, pain reports) which can be controlled by reinforcers (e.g. attention, medications, etc.) if the reinforcers are given contingent on the pain behaviours. Fordyce and his associates (see Fordyce, 1976, 1982) have consequently developed a treatment package based on operant principles. This programme concentrates on decreasing medication intake, pain levels and pain behaviours, as well as on increasing activity and other more constructive behaviours.

Activity levels are increased by systematically reinforcing gradual increases with social praise and the chance to rest. Medications are gradually decreased by giving the patient progressively smaller doses in a 'pain cocktail' which is given on a fixed time rather than pain basis. Finally, the staff and the family are trained not to reinforce pain behaviours by providing, for example, sympathy or a reduction of work responsibilities contingent on pain. The subjective experience of pain is dealt with only in the sense that pain behaviour maybe ignored and 'well' behaviour reinforced.

Quality

As seen in Table 1, a majority of the 15 studies used the rather weak one-group pre-/ post-test design. There are several problems (e.g. controlling for history, maturation, regression, and reactivity to measurement) with this design which makes causal inference difficult (Cook & Campbell, 1979). Also of particular importance in this type of research are factors extraneous to the actual treatment like placebo, attention and demand characteristics which cannot be accounted for in a one group pre-/ post-test design. Even if statistically significant differences between pre- and post-test are found, it is impossible to attribute the change as being due to the specific treatment unless there is a convincing control condition.

Table 1. Outcome studies using the operant approach

Study	*n*	Pain	Treatments	Design	Follow-up	Results
Fordyce *et al.* (1968)	3	Low back	In-patient operant programme with systematic activity increases and medication decreases	Single Sub AB	None	Increased walking and activity levels, decreased medication use
Fordyce *et al.* (1973)	36	Majority low back	Same as Fordyce (1968)	1 group pre/post	22mo.	Increased activity (S), decreased medications (S) and pain (S). At follow-up activity and pain gains maintained
Greenhoot & Sternbach (1974)	54	Diverse	In-patient programme similar to Fordyce	1 group pre/post	None	Increased activity, decreased pain

Study	n	Pain	Treatments	Design	Follow-up	Results
Sternbach (1974)	75	Diverse mostly low back	Similar to Fordyce, 25 patients also received surgery	1 group pre/post	6mo.	Increased activity (S), decreased medications (S), and pain (S). Gains maintained at follow-up
Fowler (1975)	36	Low back	As in Fordyce (1973)	1 group pre/post	Not stated	Medication intake decreased, increased activity
Cairns et al. (1976)	100	Back	Similar to Fordyce	1 group pre/post	10mo.	At follow-up 58% of the patients had decreased medication levels and 70% had decreased pain or increased activity
Swanson et al. (1976)	50	72% = back	Similar to Fordyce Some group and relaxation therapy	1 group pre/post	6mo.	At discharge activity increased 16%, pain decreased 14% and 79% of the patients decreased their medication use. At follow-up 50% deemed to have moderate or better improvement
Anderson et al. (1977)	34	79% = back	Similar to Fordyce	1 group pre/post	6mo.	Of original patients 54% rejected, 38% refused and 8% dropped out of treatment. 78% of those completing the programme had normal levels of drug use and activity
Cairns & Pasino (1977)	9	Back	In-patient activity training. 1 = no special training, 2 = verbal reinforcement, 3 = verbal reinforcement + graphic feedback	3 group pre/post	None	3 = 2>1(S) for specified activities in physical therapy
Ignelzi et al. (1977)	54	Diverse	Follow-up of Greenhoot & Sternbach (1974)	1 group follow-up	36mo.	Increased activity (S), decreased medication (S), decreased pain (S), but for those not receiving surgery pain decrease was not significant
Hammonds et al. (1978)	61	70% = low back	Analgesic nerve blocks contingent upon successful increase in weekly activity level	1 group pre/post	4wk	About 30% dropped out. Of those completing, activity levels doubled. Maintained at follow-up
Swanson et al. (1979)	200	Back, neck	In-patient programme like Swanson et al. (1976)	1 group pre/post	12mo.	18% drop-out rate. At discharge activity increased (S), 59% of patients improved medication level, decreased pain (S). At follow-up, pain decrease maintained, 20% working, 29% adhered to drug programme

Study	n	Pain	Treatments	Design	Follow-up	Results
Götestam & Mellgren (in press)	5	Diverse	Similar to Fordyce	Single sub AB	3–7mo.	Increased activity for 2 of 4 patients, Decreased medication for 4 of 5, and decreased pain for 2 of 4 patients. Gains maintained at follow-up
Roberts & Reinhardt (1980)	58	Diverse	1 = Similar to Fordyce, 2 = pts. rejected for treatment, 3 = pts. refusing treatment	3 group pre/post	1–8yr	77% of operant patients functioning normally at follow-up. 1>2, 3(S) up-time, work, drug use, and pain
Varni et al. (1980)	1	Chronic pain (burn)	Reinforced 'well' behaviour and systematic activity increases	Multiple base-line across settings, reversals	None	Observed pain behaviours decreased contingent on reinforcement of 'well' behaviours and activity increased only when treatment present

Note. S = statistically significant. Other studies using operant methods: from Table 4, Seres & Newman (1976), Seres *et al.* (1977), Newman *et al.* (1978), DeBenedittis (1979), Hudgens (1979), Block *et al.* (1980), Timming *et al.* (1980), Chapman *et al.* (1981), Malec *et al.* (1981), Tyre & Anderson (1981).

Only three studies in this group had control conditions of any type. Roberts & Reinhardt (1980) used a quasi-experimental comparison design. However, their two comparison groups were not directly comparable since quite different selection criteria were used for inclusion in each group. Cairns & Pasino (1977) employed adequate control groups, but their study was only concerned with specific activity levels during hospitalization. Finally, Varni *et al.* (1980) used the fairly strong multiple base-line single-subject design.

Outcomes

Increases in activity levels, primarily measured as up-time or performance on specific tasks, were reported in every study. Clinically, and in those reports using inferential statistics, statistically significant increases were also found at follow-up.

With regards to the use of medications, very large reductions were reguarly noted at discharge. These gains were typically reported to be maintained at follow-up, but Swanson *et al.* (1979) did report that adherence to their medication programme was lower at follow-up than at discharge.

Subjective pain ratings were ordinarily lowered, but only by a moderate amount. All studies that employed inferential statistics did obtain statistical significance, but clinically the reductions were not so impressive. As an illustration, Swanson *et al.* (1976a,b) report only a 14 per cent decrease in pain ratings. Furthermore, none of the studies was able to reduce pain below a rating of 4 on a 0 to 10 scale. Consequently, while subjective pain ratings were reduced a fair amount, patients still complained of having considerable pain. Maintenance of pain reductions was reported in every study except Ignelzi *et al.* (1977).

It should be pointed out that rejection, refusal, and drop-out rates were often high in these studies. Roberts & Reinhardt's (1980) treated group, for example, turned out to be a select minority of about 40 per cent of the pain patients considered for treatment.

Conclusions

The operant programme has consistently shown clinically significant increases in activity levels and reduction in analgesic intake. At the same time, modest reductions in subjective pain ratings have usually been reported. The studies also indicate good maintenance of treatment gains at follow-up.

While the results of the operant programme have been positive some caution is warranted. First, even though a very high percentage of those completing treatment were improved, only a minority of the original pain patient population seemed to complete the programmes. Others have also noted problems in organizing, administering and gaining control over important reinforcers in operant treatment programmes (e.g. White & Donovan, 1980; Vinck, 1981). Moreover, no data comparing the operant approach with other treatments is currently available. Finally, almost no work has been done to isolate and improve upon the active ingredients of the programme.

Theoretically the data are of considerable interest since they: (1) indicate that subjective pain reports are not perfectly correlated with other pain-related behaviours, e.g. activity levels or drug taking (supporting the operant view), and (2) call into question the operant reasoning concerning pain reports. Since subjective pain reports were not decreased to a normal level, the possibility exists that the contingencies believed to control these reports were not successfully altered (leakage), that other behaviours or reinforcers are of crucial importance (e.g. cognitive behaviours), or that the pain was not entirely operantly controlled.

While no conclusive or comparative date are available, operant programmes certainly seem to help patients live more normal lives. Future treatment efforts should concentrate on shorter, more economical out-patient methods and better techniques to control the subjective experience of pain.

The relaxation approach

The respondent or relaxation approach to pain assumes that organic processes are relevant and that they can be influenced by learning. The basic idea in treating chronic pain is to break the vicious pain circle that is believed to exist. Whenever the body is injured (typically causing pain), the tendency is to tense the muscles in that body area thereby immobilizing the site to further trauma. In the case of acute pain this respondent has obvious value, but when the muscles are chronically tensed this tension itself produces more pain which in turn causes more tensing. A pain – tension cycle begins. It is compounded eventually by other problems, e.g. lack of sleep, depression, analgesic overuse and lowered activity. Treatment emphasizes the reduction of muscle tension and psychological stress as a means of controlling the pain.

In this section, studies which used EMG biofeedback or other relaxation techniques like progressive muscle relaxation to break the vicious pain circle are reviewed, and these investigations are summarized in Table 2. EMG and pain levels are the principal measures reviewed here, since many studies unfortunately did not employ other measures.

Quality

Most of the studies in this group used weak designs, primarily the one-group pre-/ post-test design which is criticized in the operant section. Some studies did however employ some type of control condition, thereby allowing one to draw some causal conclusions (Dohrmann & Lasking, 1978; Nouwen & Solinger, 1979; Stenn *et al.*, 1979; Varni, 1981; Casas *et al.*, 1982).

Another limitation of these studies was the lack of a broad range of objective outcome measures. The typical investigation had EMG and pain ratings, but few studies reported on other pain-related behaviours. Furthermore, some studies relied entirely on subjective reports or evaluations and these were not always blind (e.g. Carlsson & Gale, 1977; Grzesiak, 1977). Follow-up periods were also generally quite short.

Comparison between studies is also made difficult since different types of chronic pain patients have been used. Namely, some reports used temporomandibular joint pain patients exclusively while others had mainly back pain patients.

Table 2. Outcome studies using the relaxation approach

Study	*n*	Pain	Treatments	Design	Follow-up	Results
Gessel & Alderman (1971)	11	TMJ	Progressive muscle relaxation	Uncontrolled case studies	None	6 of the 11 patients 'improved', 4 having 'remission'
Carlsson et al. (1975)	1	TMJ	Relaxation training and EMG masseter biofeedback	Single Sub AB	6mo.	Muscle tension reduced only with biofeedback. No pain at follow-up
Gessel (1975)	23	TMJ	EMG biofeedback of temporalis/masseter. Some received antidepressive drugs	Uncontrolled case studies	None	15 of 23 patients had symptom control with biofeedback, and 4 of the 8 non-responders got symptom control with antidepressives
Carlsson & Gale (1976)	1	TMJ	EMG biofeedback and relaxation training	Single Sub AB	1yr	Reduction in EMG tension and pain. Symptom free at follow-up.
Carlsson & Gale (1977)	11	TMJ	EMG biofeedback and tension awareness	1 group pre/post	4–15mo.	8 of 10 patients had EMG decreases and 7 of 11 had decreased pain. At follow-up 8 of 11 symptom free or much better
Gentry & Bernal (1977)	2	Back	Frontalis EMG biofeedback	Uncontrolled case studies	6wk	Both patients had reduced EMG levels and it is implied that they had pain decreases. Pain improvements maintained at follow-up
Grzesiak (1977)	4	Spine	Progressive relaxation and focusing	Uncontrolled case studies	1–2yr	All patients had decreased pain and improved mood at discharge. 3 of the 4 maintained gains at follow-up
Hendler et al. (1977)	13	Diverse	Frontalis EMG biofeedback	Uncontrolled case studies	1mo.	At follow-up, 6 of the 13 patients had some pain relief
Peck & Kraft (1977)	14	8 = back 6 = TMJ	EMG biofeedback (back/masseter)	1 group pre/post	3mo.	Back patients had slight EMG reductions and 1 of 8 had a pain reduction, while TMJ patients had EMG reductions and 2 of 6 had pain reductions. These gains maintained at follow-up

Study	n	Pain	Treatments	Design	Follow-up	Results
Dohrmann & Laskin (1978)	24	TMJ	1 = Masseter EMG biofeedback 2 = Placebo control	2 group pre-post	1yr	1>2(S) in reducing EMG level. 11 of the 13 patients in gr.1 had remission as opposed to 4 of 8 in gr.2. At follow-up 75% of gr.1 had no further treatment compared to 28% in gr.2.
Belar & Cohen (1979)	1	Back	Back muscle EMG biofeedback	Single Sub AB	6mo.	Decreased EMG and pain frequency plus increased activity at discharge. Pain reduction and activity gains maintained
Nouwen & Solinger (1979)	26	Back	1 = Back muscle EMG biofeedback 2 = Waiting list control	2 group pre/post	3mo.	1>2(S) EMG and pain reductions. At follow-up EMG returned to pre-treatment levels for gr.1, but pain reductions were maintained
Sherman et al. (1979)	14	Phantom limb	Progressive muscle relaxation, EMG feedback, and reassurance	Single Sub AB	6mo – 2yr	At follow-up 8 of the 14 patients had substantial pain decreases
Stenn et al. (1979)	11	TMJ	1 = Progressive relaxation plus coping 2 = Progressive relaxation, EMG biofeedback, and coping	2 group pre/post	3mo.	EMG levels decreased (S) 1 = 2, pain decreased (S) 2>1(S), and symptoms decreased (S) 1 = 2. Both groups maintained EMG decreases and symptom improvements at follow-up
Freeman et al. (1980)	8	Low back	EMG biofeedback	1 group pre/post	3mo.	At follow-up, 5 of the 8 patients approached a 50% reduction in EMG levels, 4 of 8 had less pain, and 5 of 8 had improved MMPI
Jones & Wolf (1980)	1	Back	Back muscle EMG biofeedback	Uncontrolled case study	5wk	At follow-up decreased EMG, pain, and drug intake levels
Nigl & Fisher (1980)	4	Back	Back muscle EMG biofeedback and relaxation training	Single Sub AB	None	Decreased EMG and pain levels observed
Todd & Belar (1980)	1	Low back	EMG back muscle biofeedback, relaxation training, and stress inoculation	Single Sub AB	None	Depression improved, but EMG and pain levels were unchanged
Varni (1981)	3	Arthritis	Progressive muscle relaxation, breathing exercises, and guided imagery	Single Sub AB with multiple base-line control	14mo.	At follow-up clinically significant pain reductions, sleep improvements, mobility increases, and analgesic use decreases

Study	n	Pain	Treatments	Design	Follow-up	Results
Varni et al. (1981)	1	Arthritic and bleeding pain	Same as in Varni (1981)	Single Sub AB	1yr	Clinically significant decreases in pain, medication intake, and hospital days plus increases in activity at follow-up
Casas et al. (1982)	16	Bruxism (TMJ)	1 = Stress reduction counselling 2 = Contingent nocturnal EMG masseter feedback 3 = 1 and 2 4 = Waiting list control	4 group pre/post	2mo.	At post-test 1 = 2 = 3> 4(S). At follow-up, symptoms (teeth grinding, pain) were decreased for: 1 = 3 of 4 patients; 2 = 3 of 4; 3 = 2 of 4; 4 = 1 of patients

Note. S = statistically significant; TMJ = temporomandibular joint. Other studies using relaxation methods: from Table 3, Levendusky & Pankratz (1975), Cautela (1977), Hartman & Ainsworth (1980); from Table 4, Seres & Newman (1976), Gottlieb *et al.* (1977), Seres *et al.* (1977), Khatami & Rush (1978), Newman *et al.* (1978), Gottleib *et al.* (1979), Khatami *et al.* (1979), Block *et al.* (1980), Taylor *et al.* (1980), Timming *et al.* (1980), Arawaka (1981), Herman & Baptiste (1981), Keefe *et al.* (1981), Tyre & Anderson (1981), Wang *et al.* (1980).

Outcome

All of the papers providing EMG data except one (Todd & Belar, 1980) reported decreases at discharge. Several of the studies analysed their data statistically and all reported significant decreases. At follow-up, these decreases tended to be maintained with the exception of Nouwen & Solinger (1979) who found that EMG levels had returned to base-line levels.

Decreases in pain ratings were also predominant. These decreases were apparently deemed by the authors to be clinically significant, but since the actual data were not ordinarily presented clinical significance was impossible to judge. Two studies did not obtain good pain reductions (Peck & Kraft, 1977; Todd & Belar, 1980). Interestingly enough, both investigations had some difficulties in reducing EMG levels. At follow-up, pain levels in comparison to discharge, were usually the same or lower. Some problems in maintenance were noted however (e.g. Hendler *et al.,* 1977; Peck & Kraft, 1977). Improvements in symptomatology and various other behaviours were also noted in a number of papers.

Conclusions

Taken as a group, the data suggest that many patients may benefit from relaxation treatment. A lack of data from well-controlled studies makes this conclusion somewhat tentative. However, the five controlled studies, as well as the other studies employing weaker designs, indicated that EMG levels can be significantly lowered with chronic pain patients and that these patients tend to experience a decrease in pain. This conclusion is in contrast to Turner & Chapman's (1982) statement that there is little evidence indicating that relaxation therapies are effective for chronic pain other than headache. The present review has, however, substantially more studies with this pain population and is therefore more comprehensive.

It is not currently clear by how much pain levels are decreased, if other pain behaviours are affected, or why the pain decreases. None of the studies evaluated, for example, whether a lowered EMG level was a necessary or sufficient condition for improvement. Neither has the role of possible extraneous variables (e.g. attention or cognitive ones) been clarified.

One advantage of relaxation therapies is that they are relatively inexpensive and easy to administer. While the empirical data are not yet available, the use of relaxation as part of a coping skills approach to pain, as Turner & Chapman (1982) among others have suggested, would seem to be prudent.

The cognitive approach

In recent years cognitive-behavioural therapy has become more and more popular. Among cognitive programmes, there are several designed to regulate pain. Most of the experiments, however, deal with cognitive strategies for acute pain in the clinic or induced in the laboratory (see Sanders, 1979; Turk & Genest, 1979). The differences between acute and chronic pain and laboratory and clinical situations are great enough that generalization cannot be easily assumed. Only five studies (Table 3) were found in which a relatively 'pure' cognitive approach was employed. A number of other investigations which used cognitive techniques in combination with behavioural ones are cross-referenced in Table 3.

Table 3. Outcome studies using the cognitive approach

Study	n	Pain	Treatments	Design	Follow-up	Results
Levendusky & Pankratz (1975)	1	Abdominal	Progressive relaxation, covert imagery, cognitive relabelling, drug withdrawal	Uncontrolled case study	None	Drug use decreased and pain was 'moderated'
Cautela (1977)	1	Arthritis	Progressive relaxation, covert conditioning, extinction of pain complaints	Uncontrolled case study	8mo.	Pain free and reduced drug intake at follow-up
Rybstein-Blinchik (1979)	44	Diverse	1 = conversation control, 2 = reinterpretation, 3 = cognitive therapy with pain-irrelevant condition, 4 = cognitive therapy with pain-relevant condition	4 group pre/post	None	2>1,3,4 pain behaviours and descriptive words (S). 2>1,3; 4>1 pain intensity (S)
Rybstein-Blinchik & Grzesiak (1979)	5	Diverse	Cognitive reinterpretation	1 group pre/post	5wk	Decreased pain ratings (S), pain behaviours (S), and words to describe pain (S). Pain intensity not significantly lowered
Hartman & Ainsworth (1980)	10	Diverse	1 = alpha feedback, stress inoculation; 2 = stress inoculation, alpha biofeedback	2 group pre/post	6wk	1>2 pain 'approaching significance'

Note. S = statistically significant. Other studies using cognitive methods: from Table 2, Stenn *et al.* (1979), Todd & Belar (1980), Varni (1981), Varni *et al.* (1981); from Table 4, Khatami & Rush (1978), Khatami *et al.*(1979), Block *et al.* (1980), Timming *et al.* (1980), Herman & Baptiste (1981), Malec *et al.* (1981).

The cognitive approach sees pain as an experience mediated by cognitions. Since pain is a subjective experience, then treatment at the cognitive level is deemed appropriate. If the pain is successfully negotiated, then there might be a concurrent change in other pain-related behaviours, e.g. activity and medication intake. Regardless of the origin of the pain, modifying cognitions might reduce pain levels and provide the patient with a better method of dealing with it.

Quality

Of the five studies, only one (Rybstein-Blinchik, 1979) employed a control condition, and three reports confounded other non-cognitive treatments with the cognitive strategies.

Outcome

The two earliest reports are uncontrolled case studies (Levendusky & Pankratz, 1975; Cautela, 1977). While both reported improvements, weak methodology and the confounding of non-cognitive treatments (see Turkat & Adams, 1978) prohibits one from drawing any conclusions.

Hartmann & Ainsworth (1980) compared stress inoculation with alpha biofeedback in a two-group crossover design. Analyses of variance failed to show significant differences between the groups although the group receiving alpha feedback first and stress inoculation second had the largest reductions in pain. Since differences between base-line and discharge or follow-up were not analysed, clinical significance cannot be deduced.

Rybstein-Blinchik has reported two interesting experiments using cognitive reinterpretation in the treatment of chronic pain. In the first study (Rybstein-Blinchik & Grezesiak, 1979) five subjects were provided with an educational background concerning pain, and they were then taught to reinterpret their cognitions so that they had thoughts that were related to, but yet were inconsistent with, pain. After eight weekly sessions the patients were found to have statistically significant reductions in pain ratings (McGill Questionnaire) as compared with base-line, but ratings of pain intensity were not significantly reduced.

In a second study, Rybstein-Blinchik (1979) compared cognitive reinterpretation with two other cognitive strategies and a control group. In short, she found that the reinterpretation group had significantly greater reductions in pain intensity, pain behaviours, and fewer words to describe pain, than the other groups. Because the actual data are not reported (e.g. means), judgements of clinical significance are restricted. Moreover, even though this study employed a strong design, it did lack a follow-up and broad outcome measures. All of the patients, in addition, came from a 'physical rehabilitation ward' but what other treatments and medication, if any, they received is not stated.

Conclusions

There is little evidence demonstrating that cognitive strategies are effective in the treatment of chronic pain or that they are the treatment of choice. One must concur with Sander's (1979) statement that a lack of studies in combination with poor designs and the confounding of cognitive with non-cognitive treatments prevents us from drawing any firm conclusions: clinical validity has not yet been really tested. On the positive side, Rybstein-Blinchik's four-group study suggests that cognitive strategies may be useful in the clinic and this line of research should certainly be continued. Whether the effects of cognitive treatments are strictly 'cognitive' or if they might be related to a general 'relaxation response' is an important theoretical question which needs to be addressed.

A more positive conclusion might be warranted if one takes into consideration the studies which have combined cognitive and behavioural techniques in the management of headaches. However, the usefulness of the cognitive techniques *per se* or in combination with behavioural methods has not yet been convincingly demonstrated.

The multimodal approach

Pain is a complex problem which is influenced by a large number of variables. Multimodal approaches try to maximize improvements by utilizing several treatment techniques to control as many of the pain variables as possible. These include the operant, relaxation and cognitive strategies already discussed, in addition to a wide range of other techniques.

Table 4. Outcome studies using a multimodal approach

Study	n	Pain	Treatments	Design	Follow-up	Results
Seres & Newman (1976)	100	Low back	In-patient operant conditioning plus biofeedback, relaxation, education, and psychotherapy	1 group pre/post	3mo.	Medication use changed from 87% of the patients to 5% at discharge and 22% at follow-up. Activity and mobility increased and was maintained at follow-up
Gottlieb *et al.* (1977)	72	Low back	In-patient programme of assertiveness training, education, drug reduction, biofeedback, vocational restoration, and physical therapy	1 group pre/post	1mo.	At discharge, 69% were clinically and functionally improved, and 81% were working or seeking vocation
Seres *et al.* (1977)	36	Low back	Same as Seres & Newman (1976)	1 group pre/post	80wk	At follow-up mobility and exercise tolerance was increased (S), decreased drug utilization and medical consultations. While pain decreased (S) during treatment a 15% increase was noted at follow-up
Khatami & Rush (1978)	5	Diverse	Out-patient relaxation or biofeedback training, cognitive therapy, and operant family therapy	1 group pre/post	1yr	Pain (S), depression (S), medication use (S), and hopelessness (S) decreased at discharge. Gains maintained at follow-up
Newman *et al.* (1978)	36	Low back	Same as Seres & Newman (1976)	1 group pre/post	80wk	At follow-up exercise and mobility increased (S), medication dosage decreased (S), but the majority of patients had the same or worse pain as on admission
DeBenedittis (1979)	15	Diverse	In-patient operant conditioning plus hypnotherapy and psychotropic drugs	1 group pre/post	1yr	At discharge mean pain ratings decreased (75%), mean medication use decreased (77%), and mean activity levels increased (55%). Improvements maintained at follow-up

Study	n	Pain	Treatments	Design	Follow-up	Results
Gottlieb *et al.* (1979)	47	Low back	Same as Gottlieb *et al.* (1977)	1 group pre/post	1yr	At follow-up 46% of patients working or seeking vocation and continued to use pain-control skills
Hudgens (1979)	24	79% = Low back	In-patient operant conditioning like Fordyce *et al.* (1973) plus family therapy	1 group pre/post	6mo. – 2yr	77% rejected, 10% refused and 8% dropped out of treatment. Family relations, work status, MMPI, activity level and health care use improved. Medications reduced to zero. 75% of patients maintained gains at follow-up
Khatami *et al.* (1979)	6	Diverse	Same as Khatami & Rush (1978)	1 group pre/post	None	Decreased hopelessness (S), pain (S), anxiety (S), and depression (S)
Block *et al.* (1980)	36	Diverse	In-patient operant conditioning plus physiological self-regulation, cognitive therapy and communication skills	1 group pre/post	None	Decreased pain (S), depression (S), and increased assertiveness (S)
Taylor *et al.* (1980)	7	Diverse	In-patient detoxification, relaxation training, and supportive therapy	Single sub AB	6mo.	At follow-up 6/6 had pain (S) decreases, 2/6 mood (S) improvements, 2/7 (S) activity increases and 5/6 were using fewer medications
Timming *et al.* (1980)	40	Diverse	In-patient operant conditioning programme plus education, relaxation, cognitive and group therapy	1 group pre/post	None	Activity seemed to increase and none of the patients was using medications at discharge
Arakawa (1981)	131	Diverse	Out-patient relaxation, hypnosis, reduced medications, nerve blocks, TNS and acupuncture	1 group pre/post	2yr	Patients having severe pain was reduced from 92% to 46% at follow-up. 47% of the patients reduced their medication intake and increased activity levels
Chapman *et al.* (1981)	100	Diverse	Out-patient detoxification, nerve blocks, physical therapy, education, and reinforcement of 'well' behaviours	1 group pre/post	21mo.	At follow-up pain (S) decreased, fewer patients using drugs and in lower doses, and daily activities (S) increased
Herman & Baptiste (1981)	75	Diverse	Out-patient education, group and cognitive therapy, relaxation and desensitization training, nerve blocks medications	1 group pre/post	None	Decreased depression (S) and pain (S). Improved attitude (S). Analgesic intake not significantly reduced

Study	n	Pain	Treatments	Design	Follow-up	Results
Keefe *et al.* (1981)	111	Low back	In-patient EMG assisted relaxation, generalization of relaxation training, self-paced medication intake, psychotropic drugs and physical therapy	1 group pre/post	None	Subjective tension ratings (S) decreased. EMG levels (S) decreased, pain reduced 29% (S), and 49% of patients lowered their medication intake. 63% reported increases in activity
Malec *et al.* (1981)	32	Not stated	In-patient operant treatment similar to Fordyce *et al.* (1973) plus coping and vocational counselling	1 group pre/post	6mo. – 3yr	At follow-up 57% of patients not using narcotics, relaxants, or tranquillizers; 75% employed or in training, and 86% had the same or less pain. Overall 37% deemed successfully treated
Tyre & Anderson (1981)	13	Diverse	In-patient detoxification, relaxation training, physical, occupational, group and family therapy	1 group pre/post	1yr	At discharge medication use was reduced to zero, pain tended to be decreased, and 8 of 13 were working or in training. Gains maintained at follow-up
Wang *et al.* (1980)	407	Diverse	Out-patient relaxation, medication reduction, activity programme, nerve blocks, trigger points injections, acupuncture	1 group pre/post	1 – 3yr	At follow-up 42% of the patients had some pain relief for 1 month or more, 50% used fewer analgesics, and 40% had increased activity levels

Note. S = statistically significant. Other studies using multimodal methods: from Table 1, Swanson *et al.* (1976), Swanson *et al.* (1979), Hammonds *et al.* (1978); from Table 2, Casas *et al.* (1982); from Table 3, Hartman & Ainsworth (1980).

Quality

The 19 investigations in this section are characterized by weak designs. All of the studies used either single subject AB designs or one-group pre-/ post-test designs. The weaknesses of these designs have been discussed previously. Although some reports (e.g. Gottlieb *et al.*, 1977; Taylor *et al.*, 1980) have relied primarily on self-report or non-blind staff evaluations, this group of studies tended to use a rather broad range of dependent variables. Cognitive, physiological, and behavioural measures were often used in addition to subjective pain reports.

Outcome

All of the studies reported considerable improvements at discharge and at follow-up. Such variables as pain reports, mood, drug use, and activity were regularly reported to be improved. It is difficult to judge the clinical significance of these improvements as a group, since the studies vary greatly in methodology and treatment, and since actual data are often not reported. While good maintenance at follow-up was generally found, this was not always the case. Painter *et al.* (1980) report, for example, that about 25 per cent of those being successfully treated deteriorated to pre-treatment levels. In another follow-up (Newman *et al.*, 1978), 66 per cent of the patients were unemployed and the pain was the same or worse at follow-up than at admission for the majority.

Several of the reports used various parts of the operant treatment package in combination with other techniques, e.g. relaxation to control the subjective experience of pain. The results tended to be positive and one study achieved very large pain rating reductions (DeBenedittis, 1979).

Conclusions

A broad range of programmes reviewed here have presented themselves as being of potential help for chronic pain sufferers. However, the preliminary nature of some of the studies and the weak designs in the others prohibits firm conclusions about utility. Controlled studies are needed. Another concern is the evaluation of components in each of these packages. Since several techniques were employed it is impossible to determine the efficacy of any of the components in these reports.

Despite the research problems involved in multimodal or 'package' treatments, they seem to be growing in popularity. Not only do they reflect the complexity of the pain problem, but their promise lies in combining the most effective parts of other treatments. The pragmatic approach of Azrin (1977) is advocated here: the development of an effective treatment is the first order of clinical research.

General conclusions

Four categories of behavioural treatment methods have been developed for the management of chronic pain. Although studies have mainly showed positive results, conclusions are restricted by methodological weaknesses. A general lack of well-controlled experimental investigations with appropriate follow-ups and outcome measures prevents us from making conclusive statements concerning effectiveness. As a result, none of the techniques has clearly demonstrated that it is effective, let alone that it is the treatment of choice. The research of the past 15 years has, however, provided a clear and strong foundation for the psychological treatment of chronic pain.

Taken as a whole, the data concerning behavioural treatments of chronic pain warrant their use in the clinic. The operant programme has consistently achieved rather impressive improvements with activity and medication variables and some improvements with pain ratings. The relaxation therapies have managed to lower EMG and pain levels, but the cognitive strategies — mainly because there are so few studies — must be deemed speculative at this time. Finally, the multimodal approaches have reported positive results with a wide variety of variables. For patients that have few other possibilities for pain relief, behavioural methods provide a positive alternative for treatment.

Several well-designed, controlled studies are needed to evaluate the overall effectiveness and the comparative utility of these programmes. Such investigations could employ either group, or the more clinically practical single-subject designs. The use of broad outcome measures and follow-ups is also important. Likewise, reports need to provide actual data (e.g. means or graphs) so that judgements about clinical significance can be made. Subsequently, analyses of the various components used in behavioural treatments can be made in an attempt to develop more compact and effective treatments. Finally, the role of the behaviour analysis in evaluating pain patients and in selecting patients most likely to respond to specified treatments should be stressed as an area for future investigation.

Acknowledgements

My thanks to K. Gunnar Gøtestam and Lennart Melin for their helpful comments on an earlier draft of this paper.

References

Anderson, T., Cole, T., Gullickson, G., Hudgens, A. & Roberts, A. (1977). Behavior modification of chronic pain: A treatment program by a multidisciplinary team. *Clinical Orthopaedics,* **129,** 96–100.

Arawaka, K. (1981). Outpatient pain clinic. *Journal of the Kansas Medical Society,* **82,** 292–294.

Azrin, N. H. (1977). A strategy for applied research: Learning based but outcome orientated. *American Psychologist,* **32,** 140–149.

Belar, C. & Cohen, J. (1979). The use of EMG feedback and progressive relaxation in the treatment of a woman with chronic back pain. *Biofeedback and Self-Regulation,* **4,** 345–353.

Block, A., Kremer, E. & Gaylor, M. (1980). Behavioral treatment of chronic pain: Variables affecting treatment efficacy. *Pain,* **8,** 367–375.

Cairns, D. & Pasino, J. (1977). Comparison of verbal reinforcement and feedback in the operant treatment of disability due to low back pain. *Behavior Therapy,* **8,** 621–630.

Cairns, D., Thomas, L., Mooney, V. & Pace, B. (1976). A comprehensive treatment approach to chronic low back pain. *Pain,* **2,** 301–308.

Carlsson, S. & Gale, E. (1976). Biofeedback treatment for muscle pain associated with the temporomandibular joint. *Journal of Behavior Therapy and Experimental Psychiatry,* **7,** 383–385.

Carlsson, S. & Gale, E. (1977). Biofeedback in the treatment of long-term temporomandibular joint pain. *Biofeedback and Self-Regulation,* **2,** 161–171.

Carlsson, S., Gale, E. & Öhman, A. (1975). Treatment of temporomandibular joint syndrome with biofeedback training. *Journal of the American Dental Association,* **91,** 602–605.

Casas, J., Beemsterboer, P. & Clark, G. (1982). A comparison of stress-reduction behavioral counseling and contingent nocturnal EMG feedback for the treatment of bruxism. *Behavior Research and Therapy,* **20,** 9–15.

Cautela, J. (1977). The use of covert conditioning in modifying pain behavior. *Journal of Behavior Therapy and Experimental Psychiatry,* **8,** 45–52.

Chapman, S., Brena, S. & Bradford, A. (1981). Treatment outcome in a chronic pain rehabilitation program. *Pain,* **11,** 255–268.

Cook, T. & Campbell, D. (1979). *Quasi-experimentation: Design and Analysis Issues for Field Settings.* Chicago: Rand McNally.

De Benedittis, G. (1979). A new strategy for chronic pain control: Preliminary results (part II). *Journal of Neurosurgical Sciences,* **23,** 191–200.

Dohrmann, R. & Laskin, D. (1978). An evaluation of electromyographic biofeedback in the treatment of myofascial pain-dysfunction syndrome. *Journal of the American Dental Association,* **96,** 656–662.

Fordyce, W. (1976). *Behavioral Methods for Chronic Pain and Illness.* St Louis: Mosby.

Fordyce, W. (1982). A behavioural perspective on chronic pain. *British Journal of Clinical Psychology,* **21,** 313–320.

Fordyce, W., Fowler, R. Lehmann, J. & DeLateur, B. (1968). Some implications of learning in problems of chronic pain. *Journal of Chronic Disease,* **21,** 179–190.

Fordyce, W., Fowler, R., Lehmann, J., DeLateur, B., Sand, P. & Trieschmann, R. (1973). Operant conditioning in the treatment of chronic pain. *Archives of Physical Medicine and Rehabilitation,* **54,** 399–408.

Fowler, R. (1975). Operant therapy for headaches. *Headache,* **15,** 63–68.

Freeman, C., Calsyn, D., Paige, A. & Halar, E. (1980). Biofeedback with low back pain patients. *American Journal of Clinical Biofeedback,* **3,** 118–122.

Gentry, W. & Bernal, G. (1977). Chronic pain. In R. Williams & W. Gentry (eds), *Behavioral Approaches to Medical Treatments.* Cambridge, MA: Ballinger.

Gessel, A. (1975). Electromyographic biofeedback and tricyclic antidepressants in myofascial pain-dysfunction syndrome. *Journal of the American Dental Association,* **91,** 1048–1052.

Gessel, A. & Alderman, M. (1971). Management of myofascial pain dysfunction syndrome of the temporomandibular joint by tension control. *Psychosomatics,* **12,** 302–309.

Götestam, K. & Mellgren, S. (in press). Psychological aspects of the treatment of chronic pain: Theoretical considerations and a series of case studies. *Tidskrift for den Norske Laegeforening.*

Gottlieb, H., Alperson, B., Koller, R. & Hockersmith, V. (1979). An innovative program for the restoration of patients with chronic back pain. *Physical Therapy,* **59,** 996–999.

Gottlieb, H., Strite, L., Koller, R. Madorsky, A., Hockersmith, V., Kleeman, M. & Wagner, J. (1977). Comprehensive rehabilitation of patients having chronic low back pain. *Archives of Physical Medicine and Rehabilitation,* **58,** 101–108.

Greenhoot, J. & Sternbach, R. (1974). Conjoint treatment of chronic pain. In J. Bonica (ed.), *Advances in Neurology: Pain,* vol. 4. New York: Raven Press.

Grzesiak, R. (1977). Relaxation techniques in the treatment of chronic pain. *Archives of Physical Medicine and Rehabilitation,* **58,** 302–304.

Hammonds, W., Brena, S. & Unikel, I. (1978). Compensation for work-related injuries and rehabilitation of patients with chronic pain. *Southern Medical Journal,* **71,** 664–666.

Hartman, L. & Ainsworth, K. (1980). Self-regulation of chronic pain. *Canadian Journal of Psychiatry,* **25**, 38–43.

Hendler, H., Derogatis, L., Avella, J. & Long, D. (1977). EMG biofeedback in patients with chronic pain. *Diseases of the Nervous System,* **38**, 505–509.

Herman, E. & Baptiste, S. (1981). Pain control: Mastery through group experience. *Pain,* **10**, 79–86.

Hudgens, A. (1979). Family-oriented treatment of chronic pain. *Journal of Marital and Family Therapy,* **5**, 67–78.

Ignelzi, R., Sternbach, R. & Timmermans, G. (1977). The pain ward follow-up analyses. *Pain,* **3**, 277–280.

Jones, A. & Wolf, S. (1980). Treating chronic low back pain. *Physical Therapy,* **60**, 58–63.

Keefe, F., Block, A., Williams, R. & Surwit, R. (1981). Behavioral treatments of chronic low back pain: Clinical outcome and individual differences in pain relief. *Pain,* **11**, 221–231.

Khatami, M. & Rush, J. (1978). A pilot study of the treatment of outpatients with chronic pain. *Pain,* **5**, 163–172.

Khatami, M., Woody, G. & O'Brien, C. (1979). Chronic pain and narcotic addiction: A multitherapeutic approach. *Comprehensive Psychiatry,* **20**, 55–60.

Levendusky, P. & Pankratz, L. (1975). Self-control techniques as an alternative to pain medication. *Journal of Abnormal Psychology,* **84**, 165–168.

Malec, J., Cayner, J., Harvey, R. & Timming, R. (1981). Pain management: Long-term follow-up of an inpatient program. *Archives of Physical Medicine and Rehabilitation,* **62**, 369–372.

Newman, R., Seres, J., Yospe, L. & Garlington, B. (1978). Multidisciplinary treatment of chronic pain: Long-term follow-up of low back pain patients. *Pain,* **4**, 283–292.

Nigl, A. & Fisher, M. (1980). Treatment of low back strain with electromyographic biofeedback and relaxation training. *Psychosomatics,* **21**, 496–499.

Nouwen, A. & Solinger, J. (1979). The effectiveness of EMG biofeedback training in low back pain. *Biofeedback and Self-Regulation,* **4**, 103–111.

Painter, J., Seres, J. & Newman, R. (1980). Assessing benefits of the pain center: Why some patients regress. *Pain,* **8**, 101–113.

Peck, C. & Kraft, G. (1977). Elctromyographic biofeedback for pain related to muscle tension. *Archives of Surgery,* **112**, 889–895.

Roberts, A. & Reinhardt, L. (1980). The behavioral management of chronic pain: Long-term follow-up with comparison groups. *Pain,* **8**, 151–162.

Rybstein-Blinchik, E. (1979). Effects of different cognitive strategies on chronic pain experience. *Journal of Behavioral Medicine,* **2**, 93–101.

Rybstein-Blinchik, E. & Grzesiak, R. (1979). Reinterpretative cognitive strategies in chronic pain management. *Archives of Physical Medicine and Rehabilitation,* **60**, 609–612.

Sanders, S. (1979). Behavioral assessment and treatment of clinical pain. In M. Hersen, R. Eisler & P. Miller (eds), *Progress in Behavior Modification,* vol 8. New York: Academic Press.

Seres, J. & Newman, R. (1976). Results of chronic low-back pain at the Portland Pain Center. *Journal of Neurosurgery,* **45**, 32–36.

Seres, J., Newman, R., Yospe, L. & Garlington, B. (1977). Evaluation and management of chronic pain by nonsurgical means. In J. Lee (ed.), *Pain Management.* Baltimore: Williams & Wilkins.

Shealy, C. & Shealy, M. (1976). Behavioral techniques in the control of pain. In M. Weisenberg & B. Tursky (eds), *Pain: New Perspectives in Therapy and Research.* New York: Plenum.

Sherman, R., Gall, N. & Gormly, J. (1979). Treatment of phantom limb pain with muscular relaxation training to disrupt the pain–anxiety–tension cycle. *Pain,* **6**, 47–55.

Stenn, P., Mothersill, K. & Brooke, R. (1979). Biofeedback and a cognitive behavioral approach to the treatment of myofascial pain dysfunction syndrome. *Behavior Therapy,* **10**, 29–36.

Sternbach, R. (1974). *Pain Patients: Traits and Treatment.* London: Academic Press.

Swanson, D., Swenson W., Maruta, T. & McPhee, M. (1976*a*). Program for managing chronic pain: I program descriptions and characteristics of patients. *Mayo Clinic Proceedings,* **51**, 401–408.

Swanson, D., Floreen, A. & Swenson, W. (1976*b*). Program for managing chronic pain: II short term results. *Mayo Clinic Proceedings,* **51**, 409–411.

Swanson, D., Maruta, T. & Swenson, W. (1979). Results of behavior modification in the treatment of chronic pain. *Psychosomatic Medicine,* **41**, 55–61.

Taylor, C., Zlutnick, S., Corley, M. & Flora, J. (1980). The effects of detoxification, relaxation, and brief supportive therapy on chronic pain. *Pain,* **8**, 319–329.

Timming, R., Cayner, J., Malec, J., Harvey, R., Schwettmann, K. & Chosey, J. (1980). Inpatient treatment program for chronic pain. *Wisconsin Medical Journal,* **79**, 23–26.

Todd, J. & Belar, C. (1980). EMG biofeedback and chronic low back pain. *American Journal of Clinical Biofeedback,* **3**, 114–117.

Turk, D. & Genest, M. (1979). Regulation of pain: The application of cognitive and behavioral techniques for prevention and remediation. In P.C. Kendall & S.D. Hollon (eds), *Cognitive-Behavioral Interventions: Theory, Research and Procedures.* New York: Academic Press.

Turkat, I. & Adams, H. (1978). Issues in pain modification: The Cautela model. *Journal of Behavior Therapy and Experimental Psychiatry,* **9**, 135–138.

Turner, J. & Chapman, C. (1982). Psychological interventions for chronic pain: A critical review (I, II). *Pain,* **12**, 1–46.

Tyre, T. & Anderson, D. (1981). Inpatient management of the chronic pain patient: One-year follow-up study. *The Journal of Family Practice,* **12**, 819–827.

Varni, J. (1981). Self-regulation techniques in the management of chronic arthritic pain in Hemophilia. *Behavior Therapy,* **12**, 185–194.

Varni, J., Bessman, C., Russo, D. & Cataldo, M. (1980). Behavioral management of chronic pain in children. *Archives of Phsycial Medicine and Rehabilitation,* **61**, 375–378.

Varni, J., Gilbert, A. & Dietrich, S. (1981). Behavioral medicine in pain and analgesia managment for the hemophilic child with factor VIII inhibitor. *Pain,* **11**, 121–126.

Vinck, J. (1981). A critical discussion of the operant approach to chronic pain. Paper presented at the International Congress of Behavior Therapy, Trondheim, Norway, 1981.

Wang, J., Ilstrup, D., Nauss, L., Nelson, D. & Wilson, P. (1980). Outpatient pain clinic: A long-term follow-up study. *Minnesota Medicine,* **63**, 663–666.

White, B. & Donovan, A. (1980). A comprehensive programme for the assessment and treatment of low back pain in Western Australia. In C. Peck & M. Wallace (eds), *Problems in Pain.* New York: Pergamon.

Received 9 February 1982; revised version received 27 April 1982

Requests for reprints should be addressed to Steven James Linton, Department of Applied Psychology, Uppsala University, Box 1225, S-75142 Uppsala, Sweden.

British Journal of Clinical Psychology (1982), **21**, 339–349   *Printed in Great Britain*

The McGill Pain Questionnaire: A replication of its construction

A. E. Reading, B. S. Everitt and C. M. Sledmere

The McGill Pain Questionnaire is in widespread use as a means of understanding the pain patient and monitoring treatment response. The current study consists of a replication of the construction of the questionnaire through the use of maximally dissimilar methodology and statistical techniques. The study comprised two stages: (*a*) an attempt to replicate the grouping of words within the questionnaire; and (*b*) an investigation of the intensity relationships of words within each subgroup. A direct grouping technique was used for stage (*a*), whereby 90 subjects sorted the words into semantically similar groups. A similarity matrix was constructed in terms of the number of times each word was associated with each of the other 78 words and subjected to cluster analysis. Inspection of the 20-group solution revealed considerable similarity with the original questionnaire. The intensity relationships were examined by asking a further group of 20 subjects to rate words on analogue scales. The results suggest a unidimensional solution to be inappropriate for a proportion of the subgroups. While there was a close resemblance with the MPQ, there was evidence for reducing the number of subgroups, as a 16-group solution offered a sensible and statistically parsimonious amalgamation. The implications of this work for the use of questionnaire methods are discussed.

Assessing and understanding the nature of a patient's pain complaint is an important and difficult clinical task. Reaching the correct diagnosis and thereby selecting the appropriate treatment may depend on an accurate assessment of the precise characteristics of the pain. Attempts at measurement should consider the nature of pain, as it is a complex, subjective experience with evidence confirming that it involves variation on several dimensions, dependent upon dynamic, ever-changing states, continuously influenced by a multitude of extrinsic and intrinsic stimuli (Sternbach, 1978). Moreover, because pain relief for a substantial portion of patients is seldom total, one task of measurement may be to identify the degree and nature of the change that is brought about by treatment.

Rating scales remain in common usage in research settings, in spite of evidence that they fail to reflect adequately the complexity of the pain experience (Frederickson *et al.*, 1978). These methods supply limited information to the clinician confronted with the challenge of understanding a patient's pain and are insensitive to variations in the different components of the pain experience. In clinical settings the most widely used measure is descriptive words. There have been attempts to relate the words used to the seriousness of the condition (Devine & Merskey, 1965), the location of the pain (Klein & Brown, 1967) and whether of psychiatric origin (Agnew & Merskey, 1976). Melzack (1975) has developed a questionnaire to describe and measure pain. The McGill Pain Questionnaire (MPQ) consists of pain adjectives which provide a means of assessing the quality as well as the intensity of the pain. The words are classified into 20 groups, each of which is intended to reflect a specific pain quality, with the groups themselves combined for scoring purposes to form three categories or dimensions in accordance with Melzack's (1973) three-factor model of pain: sensory-discriminative, affective and evaluative. The instructions accompanying the MPQ permit patients to select one word at most from each of the 20 subgroups. This is intended to minimise the possibility of several words within a single subgroup being checked, where many of these will only peripherally describe the pain. It also enables precise information on intensity to be obtained, assuming the word groups are semantically homogenous.

The questionnaire has been used as a dependent measure in pain treatment evaluations (Fox & Melzack, 1976) and the response patterns have been shown to discriminate among patients suffering from different kinds of pain (Dubuisson & Melzack, 1976). However,

0144-6657/82/040339–11 $02.00/0

Melzack's (1975) three dimensions were nominated on an *a priori* basis and have been questioned by empirical studies, since a distinctive evaluative component has failed to emerge consistently from factor analytic investigations. Thus, Crocket *et al.* (1977) derived five factors reflecting affective and sensory dimensions and Leavitt *et al.* (1978) using a modified format with back pain patients, seven factors with the major dimension reflecting affective words and the remainder specific sensory qualities. Similarly, in an analysis of the MPQ responses of women suffering from dysmenorrhea, factors reflecting sensory qualities and the reaction component were identified (Reading, 1979). However, using oblique rotation, a specific evaluative component has been identified (Prieto *et al.*, 1980), although this was less well defined when the factors were subjected to orthogonal rotation.

Although Melzack (1975) presented the questionnaire as a preliminary step in the quantification of the pain experience, there have been no reported attempts to replicate its construction. The original development of the quesionnaire consisted of three stages (Melzack & Torgerson, 1971): (*a*) classifying word descriptors; (*b*) determining the intensity values of each word; (*c*) selecting those words which have the same intensity relationships within a subclass as determined by doctors, patients and students in order to arrive at the final version of the questionnaire. The present study will consist of an attempt to both replicate the content of the word groups (stage *a*) and to describe the intensity distribution of adjectives within each subgroup (stage *b*), employing an alternative method and different statistical techniques. These two stages will be presented separately.

Study 1: Replication of stage (a)

Method

In the original construction of the questionnaire adjectives were classified into groups of similar meaning and subjects ($n = 20$) asked to state their agreement with this organization (Melzack & Torgerson, 1971). An arbitrary criterion of 65 per cent agreement was adhered to in interpreting the results. This led to the construction of word groups reflecting the following sensory qualities: temporal, spatial, punctate pressure, incisive pressure, constrictive pressure, traction pressure, thermal brightness, dullness and miscellaneous; and for affective groups, tension, autonomic, fear, punishment, miscellaneous; with a separate evaluative group. In the present experiment, in order to employ a direct grouping or classification technique (Wexler & Romney, 1972) each of the words from the MPQ was transcribed onto individual cards. Subjects ($n = 90$) were asked to sort the cards into groups describing a similar pain quality. (The example Cool, Cold, Freezing was given as indicating differing intensities of a pain sensation or quality.) They were given no time limit nor was the number of groups to be used specified. Subjects were Caucasian to exclude the possibility of ethnic variation in the use of pain descriptors (Mechanic, 1978), with 62 women and 28 men. The mean time taken to complete the task was 31 minutes with a range of 15 to 70 minutes. The mean number of groups was 19 with a range from 7 to 31.

Analysis

Assessment of similarity between adjectives. The first step in the analysis was to convert the raw data into a matrix of similarities between each pair of pain adjectives. The measure of similarity chosen is derived from principles of information theory and has been described previously (Burton, 1972). Each subject was allowed to sort the words into any number of groups and we shall represent the number of groups given by the *i*th subject as N_i with N_{ij} denoting the number of words in the *j*th group for this subject. The probability that two words are placed in the same group, *j,* by this subject, given that we have no information about which words have been placed in the group is given by

$$P_{ij} = \frac{N_{ij}\,(N_{ij} - 1)}{N_w\,(N_w - 1)} \tag{1}$$

where N_w is the total number of words. The probability that two words are placed in different groups by subject i is obtained as

$$Q_i = 1 \cdot 0 - \sum_{j=1}^{N_{ij}} P_{ij} \qquad (2)$$

The 'information content' of the events, 'two words are in the same group' and 'two words are in different groups', for this particular subject is given by the negative of the logarithm to the base two of P_{ij} and Q_i respectively (see, for example, Siegel, 1956).

The similarity measure used allows the first of these events to count as a positive increment to the degree of similarity of the two words, and the second a decrement. However, in order to weight all subjects equally, it is necessary to normalize the proposed increases and decreases using the mean and sum of squares of these for each subject; in this way the final similarity measure for adjectives k and l, Z_{kl}, is given by

$$Z_{kl} = \sum_{i=1}^{N} \left[\frac{X_{ikl} - E_i}{S_i} \right] \qquad (3)$$

where N is the number of subjects and X_{ikl} is given by

$$X_{ikl} = \begin{cases} - \log_2 P_{ij} \\ \\ + \log_2 Q_i \end{cases} \text{where words } k \text{ and } l \begin{cases} \text{are both placed in} \\ \text{groups} \\ \\ \text{are placed} \\ \text{in different groups} \end{cases} \text{by subject } i$$

and E_i and S_i are the mean and 'sum of squares' terms given by

$$E_i = - \left(\sum_{j=1}^{N_i} P_{ij} \log_2 P_{ij} \right) + Q_i \log_2 Q_i, \qquad (4)$$

$$S_i = \left(\sum_{j=1}^{N_{ij}} P_{ij} \left[\log_2 P_{ij} \right]^2 \right) + Q_i \left[\log_2 Q_i \right]^2. \qquad (5)$$

The rationale behind this measure is that when a subject places two words in a very small group the event has high information and there is, consequently, a relatively large increment to the appropriate similarity; on the other hand, when two words are placed together in a fairly large group, then there will be only a small increase in the similarity if Q_i is small (that is, there is a low probability of a given two words being in different groups), and a smaller decrease if Q_i is large. In this way the measure compensates for differences among subjects in the sizes of the groups produced.

Analysis of the similarity matrix: (1) non-metric multidimensional scaling. The similarity matrix derived as described above was first subjected to non-metric multidimensional scaling (Kruskal, 1964) in an attempt to uncover the main dimensions underlying the judgements of similarity between the pain adjectives. The MDSCAL computer program was used for this purpose and solutions were obtained for five down to one dimension.

(2) Cluster analyses of the similarity matrix. The final step in the analysis was to subject the matrix of similarities between the pain adjectives to two methods of hierarchic cluster analysis, complete linkage and group average (Everitt, 1980).

Table 1. Comparison of the McGill Pain Questionnaire with the 20-group solution

McGill Pain Questionnaire				20-group solution			
1 Flickering Quivering Pulsing Throbbing Beating	**2** Jumping Flashing Shooting	**3** Pricking Boring Drilling Stabbing Lancinating	**4** Sharp Cutting Lacerating	**1** Flickering Quivering Jumping Pulsing Flashing Throbbing Beating Pounding Shooting (Spatiotemporal)	**2** Boring Penetrating Drilling Piercing (Punctate pressure)	**3** Sharp Lancinating Cutting Stabbing Lacerating (Incisive pressure)	**4** Pressing Heavy Suffocating Crushing (Cumulative pressure)
5 Pinching Pressing Gnawing Cramping Crushing	**6** Tugging Pulling Wrenching	**7** Hot Burning Scalding Searing	**8** Tingling Itchy Smarting Stinging	**5** Pinching Squeezing (Constrictive pressure)	**6** Rasping Gnawing (Gnawing)	**7** Aching Cramping (Cramping)	**8** Pulling Drawing Wrenching Tugging Tearing (Traction pressure)
9 Dull Sore Hurting Aching Heavy	**10** Tender Taut Rasping Splitting	**11** Tiring Exhausting	**12** Sickening Suffocating	**9** Hot Burning Searing Scalding (Thermal)	**10** Tingling Itchy Pricking Smarting Stinging (Brightness)	**11** Cool Numb Dull Cold Freezing (Dull)	**12** Tight Taut (Tightness)
13 Fearful Frightful Terrifying	**14** Punishing Gruelling Cruel Vicious Killing	**15** Wretched Blinding	**16** Annoying Troublesome Miserable Intense Unbearable	**13** Spreading Radiating (Spatial)	**14** Tender Sore Hurting (General sensory)	**15** Tiring Exhausting (Tiring)	**16** Nauseating Sickening (Sickening)
17 Spreading Radiating Penetrating Piercing	**18** Tight Numb Drawing Squeezing Tearing	**19** Cool Cold Freezing	**20** Nagging Nauseating Agonizing Dreadful Torturing	**17** Splitting Blinding	**18** Troublesome Annoying Nagging Miserable Wretched (Nagging)	**19** Intense Agonizing Unbearable (Intensity)	**20** Fearful Gruelling Frightful Punishing Dreadful Cruel Terrifying Vicious Torturing Killing (Fear/ evaluative)

(Descriptive labels in parentheses)

Results

The results from the application of multidimensional scaling to the similarity matrix were on the whole disappointing, giving unacceptably high 'stress' figures and being extremely difficult to interpret. The major reason for this appeared to be the phenomenon known as degeneracy (Kruskal & Wish, 1978), which arises primarily when the objects being scaled (the pain adjectives in this investigation) have a natural clustering with the similarities between objects in different clusters, almost all being smaller than the similarities between objects within the same cluster. This suggested that a cluster analysis of the similarity matrix would, in this case, be far more helpful, and it is these results that we report here.

Both complete linkage and group average clustering were applied to the similarity matrix and it was encouraging to find that both methods gave extremely similar solutions. Consequently only that from the group average method will be described. To begin with, the 20-group partition was examined so that a direct comparison could be made with the 20 groups suggested by Melzack (1975). The composition of the groups in both cases is shown in Table 1. Although there is considerable similarity between the two sets, there are also a number of interesting and important differences. It can be seen that groups (1) and (2) of the MPQ, reflecting spatial and temporal sensations, are joined. Group (8) of the sensory brightness group is identical with the addition of pricking (becoming 10), and the thermal sensation group (7) emerges unchanged (becoming 9). The traction pressure group of the MPQ (6) is extended by the inclusion of 'drawing and tearing' (becoming 8). Pressure sensation groups remain, although their composition is changed. There are groups representing sickening and tiring features of the pain, with three groups (18, 19 and 20) reflecting the emotional or reaction component, as compared with five on the MPQ (13, 14, 15, 16 and 20). The distinction between word groups reflecting sensory qualities of the pain and those concerning the reaction to these is still evident. In Table 1 the derived word groups have been assigned descriptive labels. It can be seen that the sensory subgroups consist of the following: spatiotemporal; a distinction between five kinds of pressure, punctate, incisive, cumulative, constrictive, traction; gnawing and cramping sensations; thermal; brightness; dullness; tightness; spatial and a general sensation group. In addition, there are subgroups reflecting tiring and sickening pain qualities; a 'splitting-binding' quality; and from the reaction perspective, separate subgroups reflecting nagging aspects, intensity and fear/evaluative descriptors.

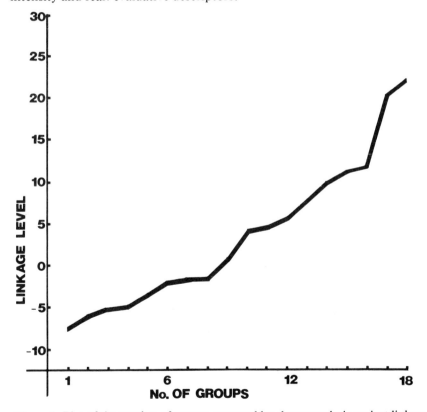

Figure 1. Plot of the number of groups extracted by cluster analysis against linkage level.

Examination of the 20-group solution produced by the group averaging clustering method allowed direct comparison with MPQ groups; however, it is possible that some other number of groups might provide a more adequate fit to the data, in terms of describing the relationship between pain adjectives implied by their similarities. The problem of choosing the 'correct number of groups' when using clustering techniques is a difficult one, has been discussed in detail by Everitt (1979), and no completely satisfactory method is yet available. However, with the type of hierarchal clustering techniques employed in this study, a plot of dendogram linkage level against number of groups is sometimes suggestive of the appropriate number of groups, by the presence of an 'elbow' or sharp step in the curve (Gower, 1975). Such a plot is shown in Fig. 1 and indicates that the 16-group solution should be given careful consideration, as the fall at this point is almost three times that occurring elsewhere (between 8 and 9). The composition of the groups for this solution is shown in Table 2. It can be seen that the reaction word groups are collapsed with a more general fear/punishment/evaluation cluster of adjectives emerging. The tiring component is combined with the nagging descriptors to form a tension – nagging subgroup. Amongst sensory words, the constrictive pressure subgroup is enlarged to accommodate words from the tight subgroup, and the gnawing and cramping subgroups are combined. Once again, a distinction can be made between sensation and reaction subgroups.

Table 2. Subclasses of pain descriptors: 16-group solution

		Kendall's W			Kendall's W
1 Spatio- temporal	Flickering Quivering Jumping Pulsing Flashing Throbbing Beating Pounding Shooting	$0\cdot58$ ($P<0\cdot001$)	9 Brightness	Tingling Itchy Pricking Smarting Stinging	$0\cdot78$ ($P<0\cdot001$)
			10 Dullness	Cool Numb Dull Cold Freezing	$0\cdot48$ ($P<0\cdot001$)
2 Punctate pressure	Boring Penetrating Drilling Piercing	$0\cdot31$ ($P<0\cdot001$)	11 Spatial	Spreading Radiating	
3 Incisive pressure	Sharp Lancinating Cutting Stabbing Lacerating	$0\cdot24$ ($P<0\cdot001$)	12 General sensation	Tender Sore Hurting	$0\cdot47$ ($P<0\cdot001$)
			13 Specific Sensation	Splitting Blinding	$0\cdot04$ n.s.
4 Cumulative pressure	Pressing Heavy Suffocating Crushing	$0\cdot72$ ($P<0\cdot001$)	14 Sickening	Nauseating Sickening	$0\cdot30$ ($P<0\cdot05$)
5 Constrictive pressure	Pinching Squeezing Tight Taut	$0\cdot21$ ($P<0\cdot001$)	15 Tension	Troublesome Annoying Tiring Nagging Miserable Exhausting Wretched	$0\cdot45$ ($P<0\cdot001$)
6 Gnawing/ cramping	Aching Rasping Gnawing Cramping	$0\cdot11$ n.s.	16 Fear/ punishment/ evaluative	Fearful Gruelling Frightful Punishing Dreadful Cruel Intense Terrifying Vicious Agonizing Torturing Killing Unbearable	$0\cdot57$ ($P<0\cdot001$)
7 Traction pressure	Pulling Drawing Wrenching Tugging Tearing	$0\cdot80$ ($P<0\cdot001$)			
8 Thermal	Hot Burning Searing Scalding	$0\cdot71$ ($P<0\cdot001$)			

Study 2: Replication of step (b)

Method

Having established word groupings, the question arises as to the extent to which the adjectives within each group reflect differing degrees of pain. Melzack & Torgerson (1971) asked groups of doctors, students and patients to rate each word in random order on five-point verbal rating scales. Cross modality matching methods have been used to verify the relative magnitude of these dimensions. Tursky (1976) produced reliable scales of sensory, affective and verbal descriptors drawn from the MPQ words. Gracely *et al.* (1978a, b) have extended this work, by investigating the relative magnitude implied by verbal descriptors of sensory intensity, unpleasantness and painfulness. Verbal descriptors were matched with estimates of time, line length and handgrip and both with an experimental pain stimulus. Relative magnitude estimates yielded high agreement with ranking methods. In the present study in an effort to extract information about the internal structure of each of the groups of adjectives determined by the cluster analysis, and in particular to examine to what extent the words could be ordered along an intensity dimension, a further set of data was collected by asking each of 20 new subjects to consider each of the 16 groups of words in turn and to position each word on a 50 cm line in accordance with their idea of the relative intensity of pain described by each adjective. The line was unmarked and anchored at each end by the words 'no pain at all' and 'worst pain imaginable'. Two measures were recorded: (*a*) the ranking of the least intense through to the most intense word; (*b*) the exact relationship, in other words, distance apart, between each pair of words within each subgroup. Thus, for group number 2 containing four adjectives, six relationships were recorded and for group number 16, which contained 13 words, the distance between 78 separate pairs of adjectives was noted.

Results

To examine the consistency of the judgements, Kendall's *W* statistic was calculated (Shannon, 1948) for each group of words. The results are shown in Table 2. For the majority of groups the value of *W* is significantly different from zero, indicating that there is some agreement amongst the subjects in ranking the adjectives for intensity. However, apart from a few groups such as group 1, group 4, group 7, group 8, group 9 and group 16 the agreement is not strikingly high.

Next an average between adjectives distance matrix for each group was constructed from the judgements given by each subject. Each of these matrices was then subjected to non-metric multidimensional scaling in an effort to assess the dimensional structure of each group. The distribution of adjectives is shown in Fig. 2. For many groups a one-dimensional solution provided an adequate fit, indicating that for these groups the adjectives might reasonably be ordered along an intensity dimension. For a number of groups, however, two dimensions were necessary. In particular, group 7 had a stress value, which indicates the goodness of fit of 38·7 per cent for a one-dimensional solution, but only 0·1 per cent for the two-dimensional solution. Where a one-dimensional solution was appropriate the scale values assigned to each word indicated that they were not necessarily equally spaced along the intensity dimension. A low stress value and a reasonably even spread of adjectives emerged for subgroups 1, 3, 6, 7, 9, 10, 15 and 16

Discussion

This study has examined the internal structure of the MPQ in terms of the composition of the word groups. A direct grouping technique was employed in order to assess the level of correspondence to emerge. The results confirm the feasibility of constructing word groups of similar pain qualities. Subjects found this to be a manageable task and the mean number of groups used, in the absence of guidelines, approached the number in the MPQ, with a range from a minimum of 7 to a maximum of 31. Inspection of adjectives comprising the groups indicated considerable similarity with the MPQ groupings. The descriptors within each subgroup were sufficiently homogenous to permit a summary label to be given to each one. It was also possible to distinguish between subgroups reflecting sensory words and

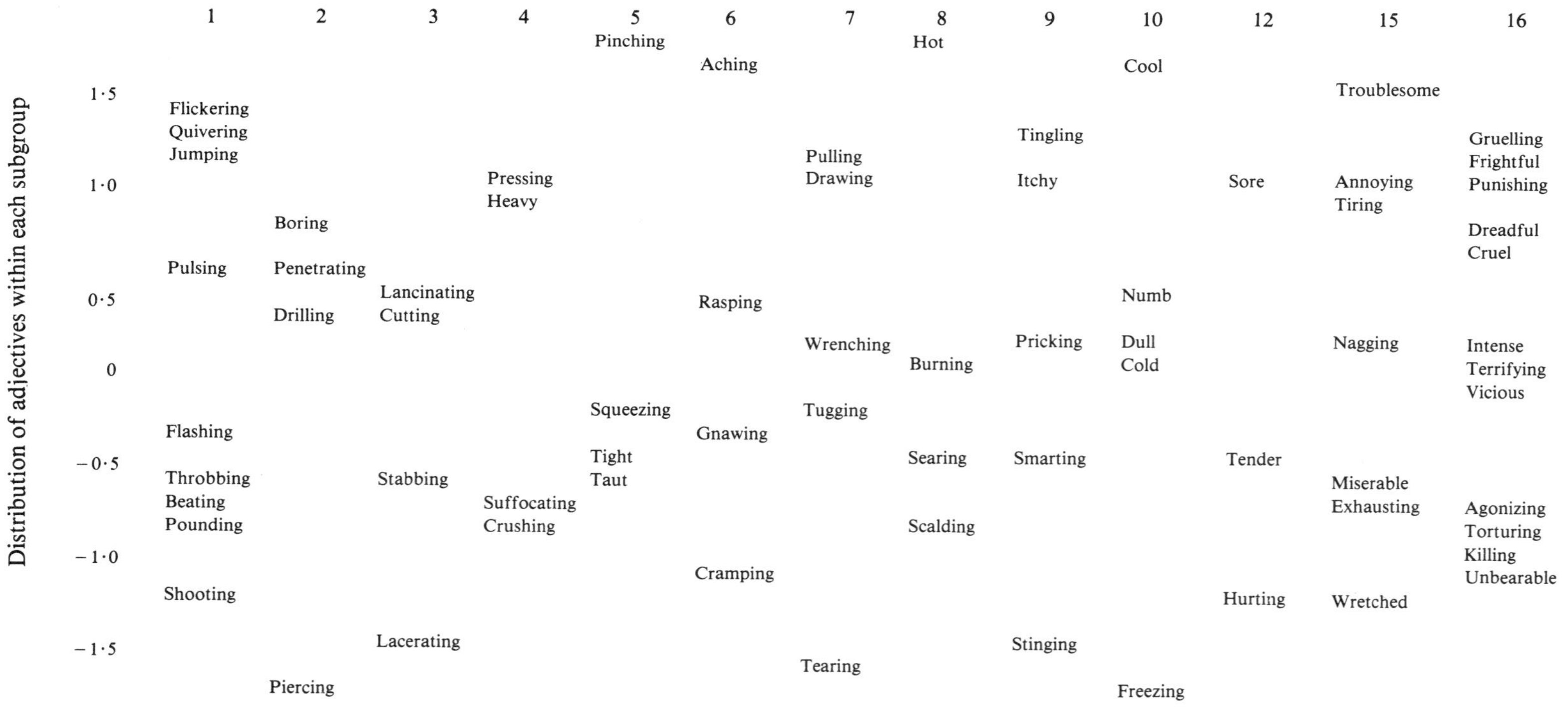

Figure 2. The distribution of adjectives within each subgroup subjected to multidimensional scaling: The one-dimensional solution.
Note. It is not meaningful to assess the dimensions of two-word groups − 11, 13, 14. Comparisons across word groups are not appropriate.

those containing words concerned with the emotional significance or reaction aspect of the pain experience. However, the results do call into question some of the original groupings, with the composition of a number of sensation groups being changed. There is evidence for reducing the number of groups contained in the MPQ. The 16 group solution reflects a sensible amalgamation of the original descriptors, since the words comprising these subgroups appear to be semantically similar. However, in view of the divergent methodology and dissimilar statistical treatment of the data, the level of correspondence between the original and derived versions of the questionnaire is considerable. Moreover, it is as yet unclear as to whether the differences between this format and the MPQ resulted from semantic differences among the subject pools, owing to their dissimilar cultural backgrounds, or indicate that the original groupings require revision.

It would be interesting to replicate the groupings using patient populations, because neither this nor the original survey studied the language of patients experiencing pain. However, such evaluations would encounter both practical and theoretical difficulties. One is the time and sustained attention required to complete the task, which cannot be assumed of patients experiencing pain. Second, and more seriously, is the likelihood that the task will differ for this sample, as they may group words, irrespective of instructions given, in accordance with their own personal experience rather than on the basis of similarity of meaning. It is for these reasons that a non-clinical sample was studied.

The results of the second stage of the replication concerned with the scaling of words are less encouraging. Overall these results indicate there to be large individual differences amongst subjects over how the adjectives within a group describe the intensity of pain, although the results of the scaling exercise indicate that for many of the 16 groups an underlying intensity dimension is not an unreasonable assumption. These results have implications for the way in which the questionnaire is scored, in that Melzack's (1975) original objective of deriving scale score values may be questionable until further work has been conducted to determine realistic 'intensity' values for the adjectives in subgroups displaying a unidimensional structure.

The use of psychophysical scaling methods employing cross modality matching may assist in defining these intensity relationships (Gracely *et al.*, 1978a, b; Price *et al.*, 1980). For those subgroups yielding high stress values for a single dimensional solution, the practice of deriving ordinal scores becomes questionable. Bailey & Davidson (1976) suggested that intensity may be more appropriate for affective-evaluative aspects of pain than for sensations. While the latter may have utility in understanding the nature of the pain and reaching a diagnosis, the intensity may be defined by emotive-evaluative words. Certainly the affective-evaluative subgroups conformed more closely in the present study to a undimensional statistical solution in terms of intensity scaling. This raises the possibility of imposing different instructions on the questionnaire for the different sections. Thus, it may be that the sensation words lend themselves to descriptive interpretation, with greater attention given to the intensity relationships of words within the affective-reaction groups.

In conclusion, the results of the study lend further support to the multifaceted treatment of pain. It appears that there is sufficient consensus over the identification of pain qualities and the use of pain descriptors to enable subgroups to be derived which reflect specific aspects of the pain experience. In the clinical setting, the pattern of words used may be relevant to the selection of treatment and prognosis. For example, Leavitt & Garron (1980) have employed a modified form of the McGill Pain Questionnaire to identify low back pain patients with serious emotional disturbance based on their pattern of adjective choice. Where a prominent reaction component emerges, it may be focused on directly through counselling or reassurance. This may potentiate the effect of drugs. The pattern of responses on questionnaire measures may also help to explain the variable response to physical treatments, as the emotional significance attached to pain sensations may attenuate drug effects. By using such measures it may become possible to understand the degree to which the pain sensations are amplified by emotional states. They also introduce the possibility of detecting specific treatment effects. Thus, some drugs may have selective effects on emotions surrounding the pain but may not abolish the sensations (Gracely *et al.*, 1979). The next stage in the investigation will be to compare the different versions of the questionnaire on clinical populations in order to evaluate their clinical utility.

Acknowledgements

This study was presented at a Poster Session of the Third World Congress on Pain, Edinburgh. The research was aided by a grant from the Research Fund of the University of London.

References

Agnew, D. C. & Merskey, H. (1976). Words of chronic pain. *Pain*, **2**, 73–81.
Bailey, C. A. & Davidson, P. O. (1976). The language of pain: Intensity. *Pain*, **2**, 319–324.
Burton, M. (1972). Semantic dimensions of occupation names. In A. K. Romney, R. N. Shepard & S. B. Nerlove (eds), *Multidimensional Scaling*, vol. II, pp.55–71. New York: Seminar Press.
Crockett, D. J., Pricachin, K. M. & Craig, K. (1977). Factors of the language of pain in patient and volunteer groups. *Pain*, **4**, 175–182.
Devine, R. & Merskey, H. (1965). The description of pain in psychiatric and general medical patients. *Journal of Psychosomatic Research*, **9**, 311–316.
Dubuisson, D. & Melzack, R. (1976). Classification of clinical pain description by multiple group discriminant analysis. *Experimental Neurology*, **51**, 480–487.
Everitt, B. S. (1979). Unresolved problems in cluster analysis. *Biometrics*, **35**, 169–181.
Everitt, B. S. (1980). *Cluster Analysis*. London: Heinemann Educational.
Fox, E. J. & Melzack, R. (1976). Transcutaneous electrical stimulation and acupuncture: Comparisons of treatment for low back pain. *Pain*, **2**, 141–148.
Frederickson, L. W., Lynd, R. S. & Ross, J. (1978). Methodology in the measurement of pain. *Behavior Therapy*, **9**, 486–488.
Gower, J. (1975). Goodness-of-fit criteria for classification and other patterned structures. *Proceedings of the 8th International Conference on Numerical Taxonomy*, 38–62.
Gracely, R. H., Dubner, R. & McGrath, P. (1979). Narcotic analgesia: Fetanyl reduces the intensity but not the unpleasantness of painful tooth pulp sensations. *Science*, **203**, 1261–1263.
Gracely, R. H., McGrath, P. & Dubner, R. (1978*a*). Ratio scales of sensory and affective verbal pain descriptors. *Pain*, **5**, 5–18.
Gracely, R. H., McGrath, P. & Dubner, R. (1978*b*). Validity and sensitivity of ratio scales of sensory and affective verbal pain descriptors: Manipulation of effects by diazepam. *Pain*, **5**, 19–29.
Klein, R. F. & Brown, W. (1967). Pain descriptors in the medical setting. *Journal of Psychosomatic Research*, **10**, 367–372.
Kruskal, J. B. (1964). Multidimensional scaling by optimising goodness-of-fit to non-metric hypotheses. *Psychometrika*, **29**, 1–27.
Kruskal, J. B. & Wish, M. (1978). *Multidimensional Scaling*. Sage University Papers.
Leavitt, F. & Garron, D. C. (1980). Validity of a back pain classification scale for detecting psychological disturbance as measured by the MMPI. *Journal of Clinical Psychology*, **36**, 186–189.
Leavitt, F., Garron, D. C., Wishler, W. W. & Sheinkop, M. B. (1978). Affective and sensory dimensions of back pain. *Pain*, **5**, 273–281.
Mechanic, D. (1978). Effects of psychological distress on perceptions of physical health and use of medical and psychiatric facilties. *Journal of Human Stress*, **4**, 26–32.
Melzack, R. (1973). *The Puzzle of Pain*. London: Penguin.
Melzack, R. (1975). The McGill Pain Questionnaire: Major properties and scoring methods. *Pain*, **1**, 277–299.
Melzack, R. & Torgerson, W. S. (1971). On the language of pain. *Anaesthesiology*, **34**, 50–59.
Price, D. D., Barrett, J. J. & Graceley, R. H. (1980). A psychophysiological analysis of experimental factors that selectively influence the affective dimension of pain. *Pain*, **8**, 137–150.
Prieto, E. J., Hopson, L., Bradley, L. A., Byrne, M., Gaisinger, K. F., Midax, D. & Marchisello, P. J. (1980). The language of low back pain: Factor structure of the McGill Pain Questionnaire. *Pain*, **8**, 11–19.
Reading A. E. (1979). The internal structure of the McGill Pain Questionnaire in dysmenorrhea patients. *Pain*, **7**, 353–358.
Shannon, C. E. (1948). A mathematical theory of communication. *Bell Systems Technology Journal*, **27**, 379–423.
Siegel, S. (1956). *Nonparametric Statistics for the Behavioural Sciences*. New York: McGraw Hill.
Sternbach, R. A. (1978). Clinical aspects of pain. In R. E. Sternbach (ed.), *The Psychology of Pain*. New York: Raven Press.
Tursky, B. (1976). The development of a pain perception profile: A psychophysical approach. In M. Weisenberg & B. Tursky (eds), *Pain: New Perspectives in Therapy and Research*, pp. 171–194. New York: Raven Press.
Wexler, K. N. & Romney, A. K. (1972). Individual variations in cognitive structures. In A. K. Romney, R. N. Shepard & S. B. Nerlove (eds), *Multidimensional Scaling*, vol. II, 73–92. New York: Seminar Press.

Received 28 December 1981; revised version received 28 January 1982

Requests for reprints should be addressed to A. E. Reading, Division of Behavioral Medicine, Neuropsychiatric Institute, University of California, Los Angeles, 760 Westwood Plaza, Los Angeles, California 90024, USA.
B. S. Everitt is at the Biometrics Unit, Institute of Psychiatry, London SE5 8AF.

British Journal of Clinical Psychology (1982), **21**, 351 – 358   *Printed in Great Britain*

Behavioural analysis and control of psychosomatic symptoms of patients receiving intensive cancer treatment

William H. Redd

During the course of cancer treatment behavioural symptoms such as gagging, coughing and vomiting often develop in the absence of apparent tissue damage. Moreover, symptoms whose onsets are clearly related to disease processes often continue after the disease has been eliminated. The reported research incorporated time-series analyses of patients' behavioural symptoms and assessments of behavioural interventions involving the modification of nurse–patient and family–patient interactions. Results showed that: (1) inadvertent social reinforcement by hospital staff and family members fosters the development of behavioural symptoms; (2) personnel associated with treatment can become discriminative stimuli for social attention and thereby evoke symptom behaviours; and (3) by modifying the social reinforcement contingencies associated with treatment protocols, the frequency of psychosomatic symptoms can be reduced without changing the quality of medical/nursing care and social interaction.

A clear breakthrough in behavioural medicine was Fordyce's (1973) analysis of operant factors in chronic pain. A patient's reactions to the aversive stimulation associated with disease processes and tissue damage typically produce significant secondary gains. The result can be the strengthening of behavioural manifestations of pain (e.g. complaining and staying in bed) such that they are emitted independently of the physical conditions which initially prompted them. Indeed, in many cases pain behaviours acquire a 'life of their own' and function as operant symptoms.

The purpose of this paper is to examine Fordyce's (1978) notion of operant symptoms as it applies in the treatment of cancer. The studies my colleagues and I have conducted follow directly from Fordyce's (1973) initial conceptualizations of social learning processes associated with chronic pain; however, they are not limited to the examination of pain behaviours. The research examines behavioural symptoms commonly observed in cancer patients and seeks to determine factors that foster their development.

The immediate psychological impact of cancer

An examination of the circumstances surrounding the cancer patient's treatment quickly reveals factors which are similar to those encountered by the chronic pain patient. However, in many instances (if not in all) the cancer patient experiences greater social disruption and emotional distress (Vettese, 1976). Abruptly confronted with the diagnosis of a life-threatening disease, the cancer patient often must undergo painful and/or disfiguring treatment which can extend for months or years. These conditions are worsened when the patient is placed in restricted isolation for protection from disease and infection. The patient often experiences real social deprivation, and the only means available to control the amount of social stimulation received is to press the nurse's call button or to develop symptoms that require more intense social interaction. Confronted with a person in such distress, the response of most individuals is to attempt to ease the patient's distress and to provide sympathy.

In addition to the social reinforcement provided by family and hospital staff, there is the reinforcement provided by the knowledge that by complaining the patient is providing information to the nurse or physician which might facilitate treatment. Indeed, the recommendation that patients engage in self-examination and that they be aware of cancer's

0144-6657/82/040351 – 08 $02.00/0 © 1982 The British Psychological Society

danger signals may contribute to an increased awareness and, likewise, expression of physical symptoms.

Another factor that may contribute to the development of behavioural symptoms is an increased sensitivity to bodily sensations resulting from the relative deprivation of stimulation (i.e. distractions) associated with protective isolation. Research conducted by Pennebaker and his colleagues (Pennebaker, 1980; Pennebaker & Lightner, 1980; Pennebaker & Brittingham, 1981) has found that individuals become more aware of bodily sensations and functions in situations in which cognitive and sensory stimulation are diminished. Pennebaker & Brittingham (1981) reasoned that individuals placed in situations where distractions are absent focus on internal stimuli and notice bodily changes that they would otherwise ignore.

The development of such behavioural symptoms is especially insidious in cancer treatment. First, as with most psychosomatic symptoms, it can be extremely difficult to determine whether the particular problem has a physical or psychological base. Second, since possible psychological bases of symptoms are typically not considered until all available medical treatments have failed, the patient complaining of pain may receive unnecessarily large amounts of narcotic medications which have serious side-effects. Third, even if hospital staff are confident that the patient's behaviour is related to the secondary gains it produces, they may be reluctant to disclose their hypothesis. They often feel that such speculation would be interpreted as accusation of weakness or malingering. Indeed, one of the difficulties encountered when working with patients is their resistance to a procedure which might imply that their problems are 'all in their heads'. Fourth, hospital staff often find it difficult to alter the way they interact with patients. In fact, asking nursing staff to simply ignore a terminal patient's complaints is out of the question and might well constitute malpractice.

Behavioural manifestations of distress

Patients' distress can be profound, and often there is little that the staff and family can do. Unfortunately, expressions of sympathy can serve to encourage the patient's expression of suffering. In an attempt to comfort the patient, those providing care may make the situation worse.

What follows is a report of a behavioural intervention to relieve a terminal patient's severe distress (Redd, 1982). This case provides an example of the role of hospital staff and family in the development of symptoms. The 64-year-old male patient was admitted to the oncology unit for the treatment of pervasive melanoma. Laboratory examinations revealed that his cancer had spread to his right shoulder, neck, lungs, and right frontal areas of the brain. He also had a cancerous tumour in the right lower neck area.

During the hospitalization his medical condition worsened despite chemo- and radiotherapy. After extensive discussions with both the patient and his family regarding his very poor prognosis, it was decided that further therapeutic efforts to maintain life would not be instituted. He was given intravenous nutrition to prevent dehydration and intravenous morphine to control pain.

The patient's complaints increased during the first 10 days of his hospitalization, and he appeared to receive little relief from maximal safe dosages of morphine. By the end of the third week of hospitalization, the patient was spending over one-half of his waking hours crying, moaning, and yelling. His crying could be heard in the corridors as well as in adjacent rooms.

In accordance with hospital policy regarding the care of potentially suicidal medical patients, round-the-clock sitters were provided. Their duties included monitoring the patient's behaviour, providing rudimentary care and companionship, and obtaining medical assistance should a crisis arise. In order to facilitate the evaluation of the behavioural intervention, the sitters were also instructed to record the patient's behaviour once every 10 min, 24 hours each day. They noted whether each of the following had occurred: (1) crying, (2) moaning, (3) sleeping, (4) awake and quiet, (5) talking with family and visitors, (6) eating and (7) being examined by physicians or nurses. Sitters also noted whether the patient was in the presence of a ward nurse, physician, member of the family or was alone. Inter-observer reliability checks were conducted during base-line and intervention and the average agreement was 94 per cent.

A relatively straightforward time-out, differential-reinforcement programme was designed (Redd *et al.,* 1979). The sitter was instructed to interact with the patient normally; and, at least once every 5 min, he was to go over to the patient's bed and ask him if he wanted anything. The sitter was also instructed that if the patient began to cry or moan he was to check on the patient and correct any problems. However, if the patient continued to cry in the absence of any discernible problems, the sitter was to leave the room and remain outside as long as the patient was crying. The sitter was instructed to locate himself outside the patient's room, but in a place where he could monitor the patient. While the sitter was outside the room, the patient was protected from physical injury by high side rails on the bed and a safety belt around his waist. When the patient stopped crying the sitter was to wait 2 min before returning to the patient's room. It is important to point out that the time-out procedures involved withdrawal of social stimulation only. The patient was never deprived of access to the radio, television, reading materials, scenery outside his window, food and beverages.

Whenever the patient was awake and not crying the sitter was to provide companionship and the rudimentary nursing care specified above. Family members and medical staff were also instructed to follow the time-out, differential-reinforcement procedure regardless of the purpose and/or length of their visit. Before the programme was implemented, the psychiatric consultant and the attending physician met privately with the patient and his family to discuss his condition and the need to find an effective means of reducing his expressions of distress.

The base-line data were subjected to time-series analysis in order to determine possible relationships among variables. During the pre-intervention base-line the patient was observed crying 48 per cent of the time he was awake. During the day he showed a pattern of alternating periods of dozing and crying, with little time being spent (less than 3 per cent of all base-line observations) conversing with family and hospital staff.

During the first intervention segment there was a significant ($P < 0 \cdot 01$, Scatterwaith approximation test using a cross-spectral analysis (Gottmann, 1980)) reduction in the patient's crying (down from 48 to 35 per cent of coded observations) and the observed pattern of dozing − crying was similar to that during base-line.

During the second segment of intervention there was a second significant ($P < 0 \cdot 02$) reduction of crying (down from 36 to 14 per cent of observation of the patient awake). The pattern of alternating the periods of dozing and crying was not observed during this period, and the patient exhibited a more normal pattern of night sleeping and occasional daytime naps. The patient also showed a strong discrimination between family members and hospital staff. On 30 per cent of 'family present' observations the arrival of a member of his family evoked crying whereas in no instance did the arrival of a nurse or physician evoke crying. This relationship between family visits and crying was statistically significant ($P < 0 \cdot 01$).

By the 10th day of intervention the patient's crying had ceased and, during the last two days of intervention, the patient showed marginally significant ($P < 0 \cdot 10$) increases in occurrence of meaningful utterance and conversation.

During the six weeks between hospital discharge and the patient's death, weekly calls to the hospice were made. Crying did not reappear nor were any other indications of severe distress manifested. The patient rested quietly and occasionally conversed with his family. As his condition worsened his cognitive functioning also declined and he became comatose two days before his death.

Support for the position that the patient's crying was affected by the social contingencies is drawn from three sources of data. First, the time-series analysis revealed a significant reduction of crying associated with the use of time-out contingency. Second, during the initial phase of intervention the patient discriminated between those times when crying would be reinforced (when his family was present) and when it would not. Third, the fact that the patient's rate of coherent speech increased during the course of intervention suggests that the reduction in crying was not the result of deterioration of cognitive functioning.

A critical issue raised in this study involves the ethics of using time-out: Should the patient's crying have been 'modified'? What right did the hospital staff have to expurgate the patient in that way? The issue really involved deciding between the rights of the individual patient and the rights of other patients. Because his crying could be heard in six adjacent rooms and caused considerable distress to at least 12 other patients, it was decided that his crying had to be stopped. Then the questions became what method of modification should be used. All available medical procedures had failed and hypnosis and relaxation were deemed impractical for two reasons. First, his agitated condition precluded his cooperating with the required training; second, informal observation indicated that his crying had a strong operant component. Time-out was the only alternative.

To most individuals, the use of time-out in such a situation is immediately repugnant. In defence of the decision to use time-out, four points should be made. First, the patient and his family were fully informed as to the treatment plan before it was implemented. Second, at no time during the intervention was the patient deprived of food, water, books, TV or any available sources of entertainment. Social stimulation was the only reinforcer that was withdrawn. Third, the outcome data suggested that the patient showed signs of reduced distress after his crying was eliminated. And fourth, the patient received progressively more companionship from his family and his crying diminished. For these reasons time-out can be judged to have been the most humane and least restrictive alternative available for the patient.

Stimulus control of operant symptoms

During the initial phases of the preceding study it became clear that the patient's expressions of distress were worse when his family was present. This type of social stimulus control has been reported in children (Redd & Birnbrauer, 1969; Wahler, 1969), and nurses often comment on a patient's getting worse as soon as they enter his/her room. The second study in this series focused on that problem (Redd, 1980*b*).

Two patients suffering from acute leukaemia participated. The first patient was a 24-year-old white male who was admitted for a second course of chemo - and radiotherapy. He was described as outgoing and friendly by the staff. Although he was depressed when he first learned of his diagnosis, he seemed well adjusted to his disease. The second patient was a 63-year-old white female referred for bone marrow transplant, total body radiation, and chemotherapy. During previous hospitalizations she received many visitors and was well liked by staff.

Both patients were placed in private rooms under restricted isolations due to immunosuppression. Each of their rooms had a private bath, telephone, television, radio, and a view of the Los Angeles skyline and Pacific Ocean. However, this type of extended isolation (more than three weeks in both cases) meant a severe restriction in social interaction.

In the first 10 days of isolation both patients showed symptoms for which physical examination and laboratory tests were unable to identify any organic or physical cause. Patient I developed a deep, raspy cough which appeared to be getting stronger, despite the use of medication prescribed to reduce throat irritation. Patient II's symptom was excessive regurgitation of saliva. While her symptom was common among patients during the first days of the chemotherapy regimen, Patient II's retching did not cease after mouth ulcers had properly healed. Nursing staff noticed that for both patients the symptoms seemed to worsen when a staff member was present.

Naturalistic observations involved obtaining audiotape recordings of coughing (Patient I) or retching (Patient II) for 60 min periods every other hour for day and evening shifts (seven o'clock a.m. – eleven o'clock p.m.) during base-line and intervention periods. A tape-recorder was placed out of sight in each patient's room, with the recorder's operation controlled from outside the room. Although it was explained to each patient that the tape-recorder would be used to help the staff determine severity of the symptom, the patients were not told when or for how many hours the recorder would be operating. All audiotapes used for assessment throughout the study were independently coded by two assistants. They noted: (1) patient coughing and retching, (2) nurse entering, and (3) talking. Inter-observer agreement was 90 per cent.

The actual intervention programme involved a relatively straightforward application of extinction and differential reinforcement (Redd *et al.*, 1979). Nurses were instructed to follow their usual procedures, but *not* to focus patient – nurse discussion on the targeted symptom. If the patient asked about the symptom, the nurse was to provide a brief answer; otherwise, it was not to be mentioned. If the symptom behaviour continued during a procedure, the nurse was to complete the required nursing treatment and immediately leave the room. However, if the symptom ceased or did not occur, the nurse was to remain in the patient's room for at least 10 minutes after completing the required procedures and talk with the patient. Each successive nurse implemented the programme until she met a criterion of four successive nurse visits without the occurrence of the symptom. For Patient I, the observed probabilities of symptom occurrence were $0 \cdot 25$ when the patient was alone and $0 \cdot 75$ when a nurse was present. For Patient II, observed probabilities were $0 \cdot 18$ (patient alone) and $0 \cdot 82$ (nurse present). Using the Standard Large Sample Z Test (Ferguson, 1959), the observed probabilities for patient-alone and nurse-present conditions were compared. For both patients the presence of a nurse significantly increased the frequency of the symptom (Patient I, $Z = 7 \cdot 5$, $P < 0 \cdot 01$; Patient II, $Z = 9 \cdot 3$, $P < 0 \cdot 01$). Statistical analysis revealed no significant differences in the observed probabilities associated with the individual nurses.

Ongoing behavioural observations revealed that each successive nurse required fewer patient interactions to achieve symptom suppression. Once the social stimulus control of nursing personnel was eliminated, symptom frequency dropped to zero within less than two weeks.

Integration of operant and respondent treatment methods

In addition to the operant symptoms just described, we have observed 'respondent' behaviour symptoms. Such symptoms represent classically conditioned aversive reactions to stimuli associated with the patient's disease and its medical treatment. Our research on this topic began with a case study of the treatment of severe anxiety following gastrointestinal surgery and has now focused on controlled experiment studies of conditioned aversions associated with chemotherapy (Redd, 1980*a*).

The case involved a 53-year-old woman whose anxiety reaction to ingesting food prevented her rehabilitation following the removal of a tumour involving one-third of her stomach. The patient first sought medical treatment because she felt weak and was unable to retain solid foods. She first noticed unusual throat sensations when she ate and would vomit approximately 10 min after each meal. Initial medical evaluation indicated a mass in her oesophagus and upper part of her stomach. The patient was successfully treated with radiation to reduce the tumour and was symptom free. She led a fairly normal life until five months later when the original symptom (regurgitating solid foods) reappeared and laboratory tests revealed the recurrence of the tumour. Surgery to remove the tumour was successful. However, she continued to complain of discomfort associated with swallowing and she refused to eat.

Although the oncologists had repeatedly assured the patient that all laboratory reports showed no tumour obstruction and a functional digestive system, she insisted the discomfort experienced while swallowing food was caused by her cancer. Despite her efforts to retain food, she could not inhibit gagging and regurgitating following consumption of solid foods.

The only medical option was the insertion of a feeding tube into the patient's stomach through her nose. The medical staff wanted to avoid using the feeding tube because it would be extremely unpleasant for the patient. Because there was no physical basis for her eating problem, the medical staff felt that the problem must be psychological in origin and that some form of psychotherapy would be preferable.

During base-line assessments, the only food that did not result in gagging and regurgitation was bouillon. As soon as she would swallow anything else she would gag and within 2 min after finishing the second spoonful she would regurgitate. After the initial assessment was completed the psychiatric consultant met with the patient for seven twice-daily 45 min sessions. During this intervention period the patient was maintained on hyperalimentation, and no medication was prescribed.

During the first four intervention sessions the patient quickly learned progressive muscle relaxation (Bernstein & Borkovec, 1973) and at the beginning of the third session reported that she had successfully tried the exercises on her own. During each subsequent session the patient was directed through the exercises and then was given small amounts of selected foods.

Nursing staff was instructed to give her her daily meals as usual and to provide positive feedback if she ate anything on her plate. They were not to pressure or coax her into eating. And if she did not eat they were to ignore the entire issue. Since before the programme began the nursing staff had devoted great efforts to coaxing her and getting her any food she wanted, it was felt that her refusal to eat might be, in part, an attention-getting device. For that reason the intervention programme included extinction of her resistant behaviour and social reinforcement of eating.

Nineteen days after the programme had been implemented the patient's condition was stable and hyperalimentation was discontinued. She was able to retain all foods and was discharged as an out-patient. Although she maintained her weight and had no difficulty retaining solid foods, she continued to complain of the throat sensation. However, her fear that the sensation meant tumour recurrence slowly extinguished and, at her six- and twelve-month follow-up appointments, she stated that she no longer believed that a tumour was causing her discomfort.

At least three factors appear to have contributed to the development of her fear. First, during two separate periods over the course of her illness, she had repeated pairings of the unusual throat sensation, solid foods and regurgitation. Presumably, stimuli associated with eating while experiencing unusual throat sensations became conditional stimuli eliciting regurgitation. Although the patient did not display panic and extreme avoidance behaviours when food was presented, she did show trembling and refusal to swallow solid foods when they were placed on her bed tray.

A second factor that may have contributed to her inability to retain solid foods was the anxiety associated with her concerns regarding the possibility that her problem meant recurrence of her cancer. She reported that, whenever she tried to eat and noticed the feelings in her throat, she thought of the tumour. According to Eysenck's incubation theory (1968, 1975, 1976), the CS (unusual throat sensation associated with eating) elicited a CR (anxiety) that *functioned* as a US and strengthened itself. This process accelerated during the post-operative period. Nurses reported that during the first few days following the operation she tried to eat solid foods, but she would tell the nurse, as she drew a spoonful of food to her mouth, 'I know I'll throw up'; 'I cannot eat'; 'it's the cancer'.Within less than a week following surgery she refused to touch any of her meals.

This anxiety was undoubtedly fuelled by her fear of the recurrence of cancer. This concern was also reinforced by the fact that the surgeons wanted to schedule regular follow-up appointments and laboratory tests. The presence of such anxiety increases the patient's vulnerability to the development of new phobias. It is likely that any change in the patient's body or sensations would be interpreted by her as meaning cancer. This phenomenon is also seen in people who have never had cancer, but have been in close association with cancer patients. Although this fear may be 'neurotic' in such individuals, it is often realistic for the person who has had cancer.

The third factor was the social reinforcement provided by nursing staff for refusing to eat. In many ways the patient became 'special' because of her behaviour and received large amounts of attention from nurses and physicians through their attempts to encourage her. Although it was impossible to separate each factor operating, their combined impact on the patient's rehabilitation was clear.

Clinical implications

The procedures just outlined have immediate clinical relevance. In cases involving diseases with complex symptomatology and/or aversive treatment procedures, the treatment team should carefully consider conducting behavioural assessments to determine possible social factors in the genesis of behavioural symptoms. It should also be recognized that behavioural symptoms are not limited to the cancer patient. Such problems may be seen with any diseases that require prolonged hospitalizations and/or careful monitoring of bodily functions.

A problem that may be encountered in the application of behavioural intervention programmes is resistance among staff and patients. One concern is that behavioural psychology represents a callous view of the individual. However, my experience is that such apprehension is reduced by a careful explanation of the dangers of dwelling on individuals' weaknesses and ignoring their strengths. A second issue is the patient's unwillingness to accept the notion that symptoms can be controlled by social factors. This response stems from the belief that, if a symptom is in some way psychosomatic, then it is not real and the patient is malingering. This problem can be difficult to handle and may require considerable skill on the part of the therapist explaining the behavioural treatment programme.

Perhaps the most important issue raised by this research is how to provide superior medical and nursing care without fostering the development of psychosomatic symptoms. This problem is complex because those social contingencies that are most responsible for the development and maintenance of such symptoms are inseparable from treatment. One option is for hospital staff to devote more time and effort attending to patients' strengths than to weaknesses. That is, they must apply the procedures outlined here in a preventative manner. Of course this recommendation is not easy to implement, given the demanding schedules of oncology nurses. One solution may be greater use of volunteers and family members in providing social support. Second, patients need to be kept as intellectually active as possible. This could involve giving the patient greater responsibility in meeting personal obligations.

Cancer treatment provides an unusual opportunity for the behavioural psychologist. First, cancer patients are often in desperate need of behavioural intervention, and it has been our experience that oncologists are receptive to behavioural consultations. In many ways, the oncologist's orientation is similar to ours (i.e. identification of specific problems, time-limited treatment, and objective/empirical outcome criteria). Second, modern cancer treatment provides an unparallelled opportunity for clinically relevant and rigorously controlled behavioural research. And third, the personal rewards of alleviating suffering of the individual fighting cancer are many.

Acknowledgements

This research was supported, in part, by Grant MH 34905 from the National Institute of Mental Health and by a gift to the senior investigator from the Holmes Center for Research in Holistic Healing, Los Angeles, California. The author expresses his appreciation to M. Andrykowski and C. Neff for their helpful comments on earlier drafts of the manuscript.

References

Bernstein, D. A. & Borkovec, T. D. (1973). *Progressive Relaxation Training: A Manual for the Helping Professions*. Champaign, IL: Research Press.

Eysenck, H. J. (1968). A theory of incubation of anxiety/fear response. *Behaviour Research and Therapy*, **6**, 309–322.

Eysenck, H. J. (1975). Anxiety and the history of neurosis. In C. D. Spielberger & I. G. Sarason (eds), *Stress and Anxiety*, 1. New York: Wiley.

Eysenck, H. J. (1976). The learning theory model of neurosis—A new approach. *Behaviour Research and Therapy*, **14**, 251–267.

Ferguson, G. A. (1959) *Statistical Analysis in Psychology and Education*. New York: McGraw-Hill.

Fordyce, W. E. (1973). An operant conditioning method for managing chronic pain. *Postgraduate Medicine*, **53**, 123–134.

Fordyce, W. E. (1978). Learning processes in pain. In R. A. Sternbach (ed.), *The Psychology of Pain*. New York: Raven Press.

Gottman, J. (1980). *Time-series for Social Scientists*. New York: Cambridge University Press.

Pennebaker, J. W. (1980). Perceptual and environmental determinants of coughing. *Basic and Applied Social Psychology*, **1**, 83–91.

Pennebaker, J. W. & Brittingham, G. L. (1981). Environment and sensory cues affecting the perception of physical symptoms. In A. Baum & J. Singer (eds), *Advances in Environmental Psychology*, vol. IV. Hillsdale, NJ: Erlbaum.

Pennebaker, J. W. & Lightner, J. (1980). Competition of internal and external information in an exercise setting. *Journal of Personality and Social Psychology*, **39**, 165–174.

Redd, W. H. (1980a). In vivo desensitization in the treatment of chronic emesis following gastrointestinal surgery. *Behavior Therapy*, **11**, 421–427.

Redd, W. H. (1980b). Stimulus control and extinction of psychosomatic symptoms in cancer patients in protective isolation. *Journal of Consulting and Clinical Psychology*, **48**, 448–455.

Redd, W. H. (1982). Treatment of excessive crying in a terminal cancer patient: A time-series analysis. *Behavioral Medicine*, **5**, 225–236.

Redd, W. H. & Birnbrauer, J. S. (1969). Adults as discriminative stimuli for differential reinforcement contingencies with retarded children. *Journal of Experimental Child Psychology*, **7**, 440–447.

Redd, W. H. , Porterfield, A. L. & Andersen, B. L. (1979). *Behavior Modification: Behavioral Approaches to Human Problems*. New York: Random House.

Vettese, J. M. (1976). Problems of the patient confronting the diagnosis of cancer. In J. W. Cullen, B. H. Fox & R. N. Isoms (eds), *Cancer: The Behavioral Dimensions*. New York: Raven Press.

Wahler, R. G. (1969). Setting generality: Some specific and general effects of child behavior therapy. *Journal of Applied Behavior Analysis*, **2**, 239–246.

Received 18 January 1982; revised version received 22 February 1982

Requests for reprints should be addressed to William H. Redd, Department of Psychology, University of Illinois, 603 East Daniel Street, Champaign, IL 61820, USA.

---

* Page numbers all refer to the numbering in square brackets at the head of each page.

SF